You're Only Perfect Twice—At Birth and On Your Resume

The Insider's Guide to Changing Jobs (The Career Survival Book)

Larry Dillon

⊕ **Strategic Book Publishing**

Strategic Book Publishing
An imprint of Strategic Book Group
P.O. Box 333
Durham CT 06422
www.StrategicBookGroup.com

ISBN: 978-1-60911-123-6

Printed in the United States of America

Book Design: Rolando F. Santos

Contents

Acknowledgments

I would like to thank my editor Nancy Rosenbaum. This is the second book Nancy has edited for me. She has a gift for taking my ideas and developing them into a logical, properly worded manuscript. Nancy has a unique talent and has been an extremely valuable resource.

I also would like to express my appreciation to my brother, Captain John F. Dillon (U.S. Navy, Retired), whose management and leadership abilities provided me with a role model in life.

Three Truths of Life

There is no need for a rearview mirror in a career; the past is history.
Every change of position is a career rebirth.
Management roles are temporary.

Preface

Searching for a new job can make you feel like the silver ball in a pinball machine, careening randomly in all directions; the flipper buttons demand finesse and the flashing lights and whiz-bangs are annoying distractions. Searching for a job can be a traumatic event, like being mugged emotionally.

Even though modern technology has changed the job search process considerably, the odds of success have not changed much at all. Yes, we now have the Internet and online social networks, but employment Web sites, regardless of their different designs and clever names, all have one thing in common: millions and millions of candidate resumes in competition against yours for that one perfect job. Recruiters receive hundreds of resumes for every listed position. The reality, at best, is that your resume may only be reviewed for a few seconds by a recruiter; at worst, it may be electronically scanned and summarily rejected. Your odds of success might be as high as 1 in 500. Are you feeling lucky?

Adding to the complexity of the job search process is the physical and mental stress triggered by these selection rituals. It's not uncommon for someone who is changing jobs—that is, already has a job and is moving to another one—to feel somewhat powerless to control the direction of that little silver ball. Imagine how difficult it is for someone who has been out of the job market for some time and doesn't even know there are flipper buttons. Job-hunting strategies and processes that worked a year or two ago no longer work in the Internet era. The number of jobs that will meet your expectations and whose skills you can satisfy is not limitless. Finding those precious few "right" jobs requires talent and tenacity.

Success is founded on serious research, planning, and preparation. First impressions are critical and, believe it or not, opportunities can be lost during the introductory handshake. Sometimes, self-repackaging is required in order to succeed. Job interviewing is not a game and there are no do-overs.

As a little silver ball in the electronic job hunt, there are a few things within your control. Your personal attitude is one of them, and it is your key to success. Keeping a positive attitude is an important survival strategy for keeping that little silver ball away from the discharge chute. One method of establishing this positive mindset is to look back at your darkest time, when you had bottomed out emotionally. You survived. You pulled yourself back from that brink and you moved forward. Focusing for a moment on that negative period in your life can help you to put your current situation in perspective and strengthen your resolve to succeed.

As a young man, my worst period was during the Vietnam War. My unit was entrenched in the middle of a jungle in the Central Highlands. We were surrounded and engaged in combat with the Viet Cong for two days during a monsoon. I was waist deep in water, holding my rifle over my head, doing my best to stand still while snakes slithered around my legs under the water. Sleep deprived, on an adrenaline overload, I measured my survival in hours. Back then, survival meant returning to dry land and seeing the next day's sunrise.

I never forgot those two days. Ever since then, I have tried to the best of my ability to maintain a positive mindset in dealing with everyday downturns including unpredictable career setbacks. When I encounter a setback or disappointment, rather than feel sorry for myself, I find and focus on the positives of the situation. Self-pity and self-doubt diminish your resolve to succeed. No matter what setback you encounter, if it's not life threatening, it's not that important. Sure, it's easy for me to sit in a comfy chair and advise you to stay focused on the goal and not let things get to you. It's different for each of us and I've never walked your particular career path in your shoes. I don't pretend to be an expert on your life, but I have been involved in executive search consulting for twenty-five years, and perhaps what I know can help you. Maybe you can remember that others have been where you are and survived and prospered and so will you. Let's deploy that silver ball and get started.

Introduction

I don't measure a man's success by how high he climbs but how high he bounces when he hits bottom.

—George Patton

I have spent the past twenty-five years working in corporate executive roles including executive search. These efforts have centered on technology positions in leading corporations. I have played a part in the rapid career rise of many individuals and also witnessed career declines when positions were eliminated, roles were drained of excitement, or the candidate's skills no longer matched the position's needs.

Failure in a position should never be viewed negatively; I believe that in order to be successful in any career you need to lose one or two positions. The real difference between success and failure is how focused, creative, and aggressive you are at picking yourself up and engaging in the job search process. Like the little silver pinball resting comfortably in the launch chute, you may not be ready to initiate a job search. The pinball doesn't get to make the choice to sit there idly and neither do you. When propelled into a job search by whatever chain of events, you have to start thinking differently. You have to learn to think like a recruiter.

Everyone has an opinion on whether getting the boot or the pink slip, or walking out the door under one's own steam, justifies taking time off to recharge one's batteries. Every situation is different, but I will tell you what I have seen work and not work. In my professional opinion, this is not the time to take time off. First, from the job hunter's perspective, once you have fallen out of the nice little daily work routine, you quickly lose momentum and it's difficult to regain it. Second, from the employer's perspective, taking time off when you are in a career change situation signifies you do not have a sense of urgency, which is always one of the top requirements sought by employers.

When I meet with candidates who have dropped out of the job hunt to recharge their batteries, the first question I ask is always what happened to them that drained their batteries. Many times, their battery drained because of boredom with their position or martyrdom (feeling their role was so critical that they could not take vacations). These are not "good" reasons. An acceptable reason might be that the job was high stress (for example, a turnaround position) and required long hours and weekends to save the company, division, or product line.

A few gifted individuals among us, perhaps 1 percent, have the unique ability/luck to master the job change process. They have the right mindset and attitude to succeed. What sets them apart is their optimistic view of life and career. They accept rejection as most good salespeople do, knowing it takes them a step closer to success. Salespeople believe you need to call on a prospect ten times before you should expect a positive response. The other 99 percent of the world is a collection of bored, unchallenged, obsolete, hapless pinballs. If this sounds like you, my first word of advice is that you should never seek another position just to leverage your current position. You may succeed in getting a counteroffer of a promotion or raise, but you will never be viewed in the same positive light again. Worse, you may find your career track in your current company decidedly shorter than you might like.

Once you make the decision to leave or it is made for you, your full-time job will become finding those opportunities that match your skill set and interests. *You're Only Perfect Twice—At Birth and On Your Resume* can help you to understand and master the job search process. Your first task is to establish the proper mindset: You're a highly prized commodity that must be marketed carefully and appropriately to obtain maximum value.

1. The Reality Check

Always bear in mind that your own resolution to succeed is more important than any one thing.

—Abraham Lincoln

The best way to appreciate your job is to imagine yourself without one.

—Oscar Wilde

Leaving On Your Terms

Everyone's career has peaks and valleys. If you are reading this book, chances are you are standing at the scenic overview of a career valley. If you haven't already been laid off or fired, you should remember that your mental health during your job search can be either your greatest asset or your greatest liability. The easiest way to get a good job is to have a good job while you're looking. Even if you dislike your job and you know it has no future, if you have a job, stay there until you find the next one. I advise candidates to get in a hole, even if it's a rut, and stay there while exploring opportunities.

If you have been fired or laid off, there are a few things you can do to survive the process. The objective is to survive with as little damage as possible to your dignity. First, accept that layoffs and firings aren't always about you. Second, accept that your job, no matter what it is or might be, will not last forever. A few generations ago, people worked for the same company for their entire careers. My father, for example, worked for the same company for forty years before retiring. These days, people stay at the same company for an average of only four and a half years. Over a forty- or forty-five-year work life, that's a lot of job changes.

Some organizations get high marks for handling people with care and sensitivity when there's a forced departure. And it's difficult, if not impossible, to know when you *accept* a job how things may work out when you leave the job. But it's also very true that employees commonly aren't as skilled as they could be in handling forced exits. There usually is a degree of trauma, confusion, and anger on both parts in a termination or layoff—especially a termination—if the circumstances seem to be unfair or arbitrary. Even people who have been through several experiences give less thought to the process of leaving a job than the process of getting a job. Losing a job can actually have a positive impact on your life if you can muster the strategic survival thought process. As unlikely as you might imagine it to be, losing a job can also be a career enhancing opportunity.

Everyone reacts differently to being told they are no longer needed or wanted. Some individuals are relieved that the ordeal (the uncertainty) is over, while others react with anger or hysteria. It's not a matter of thinking; it's a matter of reacting. It happens. For those who have little experience in looking for a job or live from paycheck to paycheck, there is a tendency to panic, which only makes the situation worse. It's easy to give in to the overwhelming worries about the family budget and the embarrassment of being out of work. Take a deep breath and do a reality check. Develop the discipline to start and stay with the job search process and you will succeed.

Forced career change can cause some mild panic and then develop into a meltdown if not channeled into a planned program. Some people react to a layoff or termination notice with the somewhat deluded notion that they're special and all they need to do is just send out or post their resume. After weeks or months of sending out hundreds of resumes without a response and posting on every job board without a nibble, self-doubt overcomes their initial cockiness.

Employers and recruiters look first for reasons to screen out candidates. Resumes with typos are immediately rejected. Once your resume hasn't been screened *out*, it still needs to be screened *in*. These days, nobody *reads* resumes; they scan them, either electronically to identify word matches, or visually to quickly evaluate skills, experience, and education. Regardless of which method is applied, your resume is likely to undergo a review of under sixty seconds. If the resume shows a lengthy time off between jobs, a question arises regarding the candidate's motivation. In a competitive market, the candidate who took a vacation stands a high likelihood of being passed over in favor of the candidate who actively sought work.

There are many reasons why a recruiter or employer might not pursue you as a candidate. Understand, almost every recruiter/ employer has been a job seeker at one time and has been through your situation before; despite this shared experience, they really don't care about your problems. You need to depend on yourself for self-motivation while keeping a positive attitude. As part of your positive attitude, recognize having been laid off or fired as a great opportunity: A kick in the pants can be a great motivator to try new perspectives and new locales in which you might actually be happier, career-wise.

Identify Your Starting Point

Be honest with yourself. What do you have to offer an employer? Why should the employer of your dreams choose you over someone else? Employers seek people with solutions to problems. What will make interviewers remember you after they've completed their first round of meetings with a dozen other candidates? It comes down to your having and expressing intelligently the solution to their problems and needs: your qualifications, skills, and traits. Your objective is to convince interviewers that you are the solution they've been seeking.

What Are You Offering?

What are your three or four greatest strengths of interest to an employer? Concentrating during the interview on those three or four real strengths will make it easier for them to remember you. Your time in an interview is limited, so painting your experiences with a broad brush dilutes their value. Interviewers only remember high points that relate to their needs.

This need to match your strengths to their needs means you will have to take some time to research the position and the company. During the interview, demonstrate your knowledge by asking about possible problem areas your research has uncovered. Then, if your interviewer provides an answer to your question and you have the opportunity to follow up, focus your follow-up response on the possible solution you can offer and how that solution is supported by your skills and experience. Be clever about presenting your key qualities and strengths throughout the interview. Sell yourself.

Remember the Boy Scouts' motto: "Be prepared." If you're interviewing for a position that requires strong management skills, prepare by reviewing the possible questions that may be asked in the actual interview (many such questions are covered in the appendices later in this book) to practice weaving the threads of your strengths into the fabric of your answers. This exercise is an excellent way to prepare for an interview.

Success selling your strengths requires mentioning them more than once in the interview. If it takes the average salesperson ten pitches to a client before the deal is closed and you only have one opportunity to interview, you need to cram those ten pitches into that interview. After one day, interviewers only remember a few things that were repeated; most detail is lost. Even the best note taker misses things unless they are mentioned several times in a conversation. You want your audience to remember the important points you have made. By concentrating on just a few of your strengths, you will find it easier to discuss more succinctly and precisely what you have to offer and how it can benefit the employer. More importantly, the folks you meet are more likely to remember you for your strength.

2. Looking Out for #1

Building a Sound Body and Mind

A sound mind in a sound body is a short but full description of a happy state in this world.

—*John Locke*

The race is to the swift; the battle to the strong.

—*John Davidson*

One of the first considerations in conducting a job search is your health. Even if you are the smartest and best-prepared candidate, if you are out of shape (i.e., overweight, underweight, or look unhealthy) you will not be competitive in the job search process. Regardless of the popular admonition to not judge books by their covers, potential employers and recruiters *do* make snap decisions based on appearance in face-to-face interviews. The same holds true in telephone interviews, where voice energy (or lack thereof) can be your downfall (see Chapter 11—Making the First Contact).

No matter what question an interviewer is asking you and what your answer might be, one question is always running through an employer's or recruiter's head: Can this candidate solve the problems associated with this opportunity? If you look out of shape or if your voice is not strong, the natural conclusion is that you have not taken care of yourself. If you don't take care of yourself, why would you take care of this important position?

I have conducted literally hundreds of face-to-face candidate interviews at all corporate levels during the past twenty-five years. My experience has allowed me to develop an innate sense of the candidate in the first few minutes of the interview. This sense, of course, is based on superficial observations. The first ten minutes of the interview is small talk, with no discussion of the position. What is being assessed is the candidate overall: appearance, self-confidence, energy level, sense of humor, and likeability. These factors guide the questioning process. If the candidate is perceived to lack the "fit" to company temperament, the focus shifts from a screening-in interview to a screening-out interview. If the candidate yields a favorable impression during this initial phase of the interview, then the rest of the interview continues as a screening-in interview. Additional qualifying questions are asked to probe the depth of the candidate's skills, abilities, and "fit."

Searching for a new job can be stressful. Stress depletes the body's energy and slows the mind in ways that may not be felt but show up in one's behavior, physical appearance, and alertness. If you are not in your best shape before you start your job search, the added stress can make you look defeated, which is the opposite of what is necessary to be successful in interview situations. If you already have a workout regimen, stick to it. If you don't have one, start one. Getting in shape and staying in shape will help you relieve stress and tension, thereby increasing your likelihood of success in the job search. See, you have a job: you are working on yourself.

Studies have shown that physical exercise can spur creative thinking and reduce self-doubt and worry. That's because physical exercise releases endorphins, the brain's natural "feel-good" chemicals. They attach to the same pain-killing/feel-good receptors in the brain as morphine. In fact, their name is derived from morphine ("morphine" + "made by the body").

In researching this book, I met with Jordan Glueck, a professional trainer. He stressed the benefits, if you can afford it, of hiring a trainer to work with you to develop a program that will challenge your body daily and keep you interested in returning to the gym. The trainer should also be able to educate you on healthy eating habits to maintain your stamina and control your weight as you exercise correctly. The dropout rate at gyms is often attributed to injuries that occur when exercises are not performed correctly, but the major reason most people stop going to the gym is a combination of boredom and failure to achieve results. If you engage in exercise under the supervision of a trainer, you increase your odds of achieving physical results, avoiding boredom, and remaining motivated because someone else is pushing you on those days you are not inclined to push yourself.

You won't be looking for work twenty-four hours a day, so you can afford to devote an hour every day (or every other day), five of seven days a week for several months, to maintaining and improving your physical and mental health. A trainer can correct you if you're doing exercises incorrectly; in the absence of a trainer, simple common sense should dictate that, if you aren't sweating when you finish exercising, you're doing something wrong. If you're reading a book while you're walking on the treadmill, you're not concentrating on the exercise. While you're at the gym, focus on the exercise; you can read the book after dinner. The physical and mental health improvements you achieve from proper exercise will be apparent to you, your loved ones, and recruiters or potential employers. Be an achiever and you will achieve; be a slacker and you will stay in that rut.

As part of a healthy lifestyle, consider starting off your day with a health shake instead of sweets or a heavy breakfast. Health shakes can be quite tasty and are a quick, easy, and nutritious way to satisfy your body's nutritional requirements. A simple mix of skim milk, fruit, and protein powder can help to energize your workout and control your weight. The main ingredient lacking in most people's weight-loss diets is lean protein. A dose of lean protein at breakfast can power not only you but your job search. Since getting in shape can take weeks, if not months, start now.

The best-written resume and high-energy phone voice will fall flat if you do not live up to the image in the employer's mind of what the perfect candidate looks and sounds like in the face-to-face interview. I have known several candidates who impressed in the phone interview and bombed in the face-to-face meetings based on physical appearance.

7

During one search assignment for a vice president of sales, I sourced an excellent candidate on the opposite coast. The candidate was perfect in experience and energy over the phone. I had him take a psychology evaluation, which he passed with no issues. My impulse was to fly him out to meet the client, who also felt the candidate's qualifications were ideal. I detected a shortness of breath in one of our phone conversations and asked him if he had a problem. He dismissed my question, saying he was just getting over a cold.

I decided to go to him for a face-to-face meeting before flying him out, because he was too perfect for the job. I arranged to meet him at the hotel I was staying at the next morning. At 9:00 a.m., he knocked on my door. I opened the door and found myself face to face with a very large, decidedly overweight person. He was not able to sit in a chair; instead, he sat on the bed. I am sure my face showed my surprise. I asked him how he could possibly handle all the travel he mentioned having done in the past and would be required for this new position, given his size. He admitted that it was an issue with his current employer and that was why he was looking for another job. The interview was over. I am sure I would have arrived at the same decision, had I decided to bring him out to meet the client, when I discovered he needed three seats on the plane.

3. Dealing with Anxiety

Only those who dare to fail greatly can ever achieve greatly.
—Robert F. Kennedy

If at first you don't succeed, try, try, again. Then quit. There's no use being a damn fool about it.

—W. C. Fields

The Desperation Factor

It's rarely mentioned but frequently encountered. Recruiters and employers sense it almost instantly when meeting candidates face to face; some can even detect it when conducting a phone interview. They sense defeat. It happens when an individual has been beaten down by the job search process. The desperation comes through in the individual's voice and overall appearance. When an individual loses his or her self-confidence and gives up, no one wants to be around that individual. Certainly nobody wants to hire that person. This desperation is exhibited in many ways.

For example, I was networking to find candidates for a senior technical position. I received a call from a senior candidate who was told of my search. He walked me through his extensive experience and expertise to the point where he sounded too good not to interview. He then sent me his resume documenting

9

his experience. The resume included a local address and phone number, which was important, given that no relocation was being offered.

I called him to set up a face-to-face meeting and discovered he was visiting his brother in another state. I decided to go ahead and have the client speak with him to confirm my impressions. The call went well and the client asked to have the candidate come in to start the candidate assessment process. I called the candidate again to advise him of the good news, at which time he asked to have the client pay his airfare and expenses. I told him this was not possible, since he lived locally and we were not recruiting out of the area. The candidate launched into a well-rehearsed argument about why, if the employer wouldn't pay his airfare, I should pay for the trip since I would benefit from his placement. I declined his invitation to pay for him to interview with my client. He then admitted to me he was in another state because he was broke and could not pay his way out to the interview. He was desperate and asked me if I would help him out financially.

In another example of how desperation can exude from candidates, even via e-mail, I offer this true story. A candidate sent his resume and I responded with the following e-mail. Note: Few, if any, recruiting organizations respond to candidates who submit unsolicited resumes.

Hi Allen:

I appreciate your sending your resume to DillonGray. At the moment, we do not have a suitable opportunity that matches your interest, but opportunities for suitable positions may develop in the near future with our client base. In the meantime, based on our twenty-five years of experience in executive search, we will from time to time suggest to you new tools that may better prepare you for the candidate assessment process.

This is the time to prepare; successful candidates go beyond just improving their resumes to mastering their interviewing skills. Several recently published books explain in great detail how to win in the interviewing process. One of them, Finding Heroes, was written for the hiring manager but also provides some keen insight on how today's hiring manager views and prepares for an interview. It offers inside information on controlling the interview through nonverbal movements. Also, included in the book are more than eighty questions, your answers to which will make an interviewer sit up and listen to your responses rather than formulate the next question.

In many interviewing situations, the decision to hire is made in the first ten minutes of the interview with the balance of time being used to confirm the decision. Unfortunately, many candidates miss this opening opportunity by not controlling the interview. Work on preparing for the interview to maximize your time and double your chances of success. Finding Heroes is fast becoming a well-worn book and management tool in several of the major high-growth companies. Chances are you may be interviewing with a hiring manager who has adopted the techniques discussed in Finding Heroes.

In the interest of providing you with real-time assistance, I suggest you get as many experienced quality individuals as possible to write a recommendation for you on your LinkedIn account on www.linkedin.com; my assumption is you have an account. Many recruiters check LinkedIn and review the recommendations of possible candidates. In a way, this is a reference check.

I also want to make you aware of an online job search service that I have incorporated into my search efforts. As you look for your next career move, you should research ResumeSpider.com to help you acquire more job leads and contacts. ResumeSpider.com offers you a time-saving and effective way to connect with multiple targeted employers, corporate hiring managers, and recruiters. Resume Spider has built an extensive network of employers and recruiters that you can tap into in just minutes.

I wish you great success in your career. I will do whatever I can as a search consultant to identify opportunities.

Sincerely,
Larry Dillon

He responded to my e-mail. The big red flag of desperation can be seen from miles away in his misspellings, grammatical errors, sloppy sentence structure, and blatant pleas for assistance.

Mr. Dillon,

"I am new to the job boards and will assume since there is no question and answer session with you or your group and other recruiters via person to person (phone); it is a mass paper shufle? The most words in a resume that matches become the best fit? I need a little help with this one. I understand that a resume can tell you certain things but I would almost want to imagine that a person with my credentils' you would at least want to talk with. Are you a retained or contingency recruiter? You probably get 1,000's or resumes per day, how will you know who I am in 2 weeks? Sorry, I am just a little confusd about how this whole thing works, I am also curious, could you help explain it please."

Sincerely,
Allen

There are times when I have called candidates to discuss an opportunity and have been disappointed to hear the desperation in the person's voice. It comes through as rapid speech, interruptions in my side of the conversation, and not stopping to take a breath. I assume they fear they will not be allowed to get everything out before the conversation ends. Then, as if to reinforce the desperation, they follow up every few days, seeking news of the status of their candidacy.

When it comes to finding and landing a new position, the biggest opportunity killer is lack of self-confidence. No matter how you try to mask it by dressing sharply, expressing an aggressive personality, and demonstrating high energy, lack of self-confidence has a certain smell to it, and I'm not referring to physical hygiene. If you don't believe it, take a survey of people you respect. Ask them what impresses them when they meet someone for the first time. Chances are good they will respond with something about

12

the individual's self-confidence and personal presence.

Self-confidence = confidence in oneself and one's own abilities

Confidence = firm belief; trust; reliance, the fact of being or feeling certain; assurance

Those are definitions from *Merriam-Webster.* I'm not making up this stuff.

Few people would admit they lack self-confidence; that would be an admission of weakness. Even so, when placed in a stressful situation, such as interviewing, the body exhibits signs that are easily observed by even the most casual and inexperienced of interviewers:

Sweating or dampness on hands or face, especially on the upper lip, is a sign of nervousness and insecurity.

Over-talking when responding to a question (this turns an interviewer off quickly under any circumstance) indicates a desperate need to convince and impress someone, and also indicates an inability to be concise, which is important in work situations. Interviewers like a concise response ending with, "Would you like for me to expand on this in more detail?" Be prepared to supply additional concise facts to support your answer, if you are invited to elaborate.

Bringing a briefcase/folder of documents to support your background without having been requested to do so indicates desperation or a fear that you cannot support your accomplishments verbally. Bringing supporting materials in case they're needed is fine; mention you have them, but do not offer them unless the interviewer asks to see them. Interviewers expect candidates to try to control the process by turning the focus away from them to their written materials. As an example of this faux pas, I offer this true story. I recently interviewed a candidate for a corporate public relations position and was caught off guard by the candidate's repeated insistence that I review his materials as a means of dodging every question I asked. He stated over and over again the materials speak for him and, if I reviewed them, all my questions would be answered. This little back and forth went on for fifteen minutes, at which point I ended the interview by telling the candidate the truth: He might be the best candidate on paper, but he was the worst candidate in person. He would have been a disaster because he violated the first rule of public relations:

listening and comprehending the question before responding.

Trying to be overly friendly with the interviewer is a way of obfuscating lack of qualifications. Job search Web sites encourage candidates to try to be accepted as a friend by getting personal and relating similar interests. This can be a turn-off for the interviewer; they understand they are being played in hopes they won't explore the candidate's suitability for the position. Understand the recruiter's role is assessing your suitability, experience, and fit into the organization; he or she is not looking to make a new friend. Keeping a respectful "personal" distance makes for a more professional presentation, which allows the interviewer to arrive at a positive assessment of your fit for the organization. Candidates who continually try to divert the discussion to personal, friendly topics rather than focusing on a concise answer to the interviewer's question raise a red flag. Candidates who are evasive are hiding something and it's probably not something good.

A resume that is poorly constructed and does not easily guide the interviewer through the candidate's career is an indication of a lack of initiative. Most interviewers spend about a minute reviewing a resume. If the critical aspects of a candidate's background are not clearly laid out, the resume is rejected. A resume needs to be tailored to the position of interest in order for a quick review to yield a more comprehensive review and, ultimately, an interview. Today's resumes can be longer than two pages, if that's needed in order to supply germane information. Still, a resume is not meant to provide your life story. Document only the information needed to support your experience for the position you are applying for at the moment. Anything more is a sign of desperation.

4. Being Overqualified

Overqualified

Being overqualified is the curse of the forty-and-over candidate. The most common disqualification cited when a senior candidate is rejected is overqualification; the employer feels the overqualified candidate will be bored and quit, and then the search will have to be repeated. While this may be true in some cases, an overqualified candidate might also quickly master the position and become an asset to the organization. There are always those overqualified individuals who are just seeking an opportunity to be appreciated for what they can accomplish and are content in the role.

In the interview, avoid the temptation to discuss or expand on your accomplishments or prestigious roles, both of which might make you appear overqualified for the position. I know, it's difficult to be humble when you're brilliant and perfect and have a long string of successes to your credit, but every word of self-promotion unrelated to the position you are seeking diminishes your candidacy. Let the employer hire you and be pleasantly surprised.

Ageism in Interviewing

Pope Benedict landed his job at 78.

Ageism is illegal but it's there nonetheless, particularly in big corporations. Job seekers in the forty-and-over category can still find ways to market the experience that comes with age, which potential employers should see as an advantage, not a liability. You offer experience. You know how to handle responsibility without any hand-holding. You can hit the ground running. Management experience is a real benefit. Be sure to remind them of these truths.

If you're an older worker interviewing at a new company, maybe for the first time in years, it can feel intimidating. You may find yourself waiting in the same lobby with other candidates half your age. So what! They will need to prove themselves in the interview, the same as you, but you've already proven yourself in the workforce. Sell yourself.

For many senior professionals, sitting and waiting in lobbies can be daunting and unnerving. It's understandable to feel discouraged as you look at younger professionals and look back at how far you've come, only to find yourself now seated next to them again. This discouragement, of course, is a self-fulfilling prophecy. The secret to avoiding self-sabotage is to present yourself as an optimal combination of what you are and what the employer is looking for: An energetic problem-solver who knows the industry and technology and can communicate effectively with colleagues of any age is a winner.

The most important ingredient is to feel good about who you are and what you offer. Assess yourself and the job market to understand and manage your professional environment. Talking with trusted peers can help you with this.

Not surprisingly, the biggest issue facing older workers is ego. It's tough to step back and realize you may be more experienced than anyone else for the position, possibly even the hiring manager, but hiring managers resent being treated as juniors or made to feel less qualified than those they might bring on to work on their teams. If not handled well, chances are, you will be passed over because you "do not fit in the company's culture." When couched in this clever phrasing, it's not ageism.

I have counseled many senior candidates on the "ego factor" prior to their first interview, but many slip off subject and feel compelled to reinforce their total expertise and experience with the interviewers rather than getting the position and letting the employer discover what an asset they have recruited. The reality is that fewer, not more, people will be impressed by an older person's accomplishments.

If you are among this group of experienced senior candidates, you need to find out enough about the company to package your experience and value to them, while saying as little about yourself as possible unrelated to the position. The focus has to be on what you offer that can solve their problems. Interestingly enough, older professionals often think they know it all and do not need to take the time to research a company or industry, and then wonder why they did not get the opportunity. Be humble when interviewing; let the employer discover your talents on the job, rather than broadcasting them in advance of getting the job and lessening the chances of being selected.

Not Technology Savvy

One concern recruiters and employers have about older candidates is that they haven't kept up with the changes in technology. Today's businesses are technology driven. If you can't navigate the Internet, send e-mail, and use Windows applications with ease, your little silver pinball will be out of the game before it has a chance to score. Some interviews never reach the second question if the first question involves technology you use to conduct business and the response is a blank stare or a stammer. If the question is not asked, you need to work into the conversation the fact that you *are* technology savvy. Perhaps the interviewer prejudged you as a candidate not worthy of pursuit; mentioning your technical competency may reinstate the interviewer's interest in your candidacy.

No matter how technology savvy you are or think you are, take the time to research what technology is currently in use. Community colleges, online courses, CDs, DVDs, books, and magazines offer an affordable range of options for gaining or refreshing your knowledge of current technologies. At the very least, you'll be reminded of the buzzwords and be able to practice using them appropriately in casual conversation.

If the technology knowledge required is of Master's or Bachelor's degree level, refresh yourself on the latest developments that may play into the position. Recruiters and employers receive many resumes and screen resumes for keywords, especially for technical positions. Make sure your resume has the keywords dealing with the needed technology. Often recruiters and employers store resumes in databases and cross-reference the resumes by keywords. When a need arises for a particular skill, they search the resume database. Nobody may actually look at your resume unless that search finds the keyword on your resume.

Speaking the Language

As interviewers, recruiters look for candidates who can speak the industry language. We expect it. An older candidate who has worked in the industry is expected to have an in-depth understanding of the industry's technology. Whether you are discussing your industry experience in broad terms or getting down to technical nitty-gritty, you've got to display your knowledge through the language of your occupation. Listen to the cadence of the interviewer's speech and match your answers to that cadence. This is like mirroring body movements (see the section on body language in Chapter 13). This sort of mirroring can be very effective if done subtly.

Look Like a Professional

Physical presentation matters. A candidate who's in shape has a look of health that trumps the age question in a face-to-face meeting. A healthy body needs daily physical exercise to maintain healthy tone. As you age, the body will naturally prefer a lesser degree of physical exercise. If you give in to slowing down, it may be harder to stay in shape. Dressing appropriately for an interview, if you've somehow forgotten the importance of this factor, is discussed in Chapter 12—Presentation Is (Almost) Everything.

5. The Resume

The Purpose of Your Resume

The closest to perfection a person ever comes is when he fills out a job application form.

—*Stanley J. Randall*

The resume is a marketing tool with one specific purpose: to gain an interview. If it accomplishes this objective, you win. If it doesn't, it isn't an effective resume. A resume is a marketing pitch: nothing more, nothing less.

A resume doesn't just point out your accomplishments; it has to guarantee that, if they hire you, they will get the benefits of your problem solving experience. It has to convince the employer that you have what it takes to be successful in this new position. From the perspective of a recruiter, a well-written resume is an exciting thing to find. At times, I am so surprised when receiving a perfect resume, I move quickly to reassure myself of its veracity.

Why Do You Need a Resume?

A resume is the only acceptable way to contact an employer. Resumes are an integral part of corporate culture. Few, if any, reputable organizations will consider you without this key to the corporate kingdom. A resume offers the employer the advantage of being able to evaluate all of your accomplishments without any guarantee of consideration.

The resume is the employer's primary screening tool for obtaining basic information that might favorably influence the employer. It goes without saying but let me say it anyway . . . your resume contains your correct/current contact information. The resume establishes you as a professional person with high standards. It demonstrates excellent organizational and writing skills. Your resume is something you can circulate to your job-hunting contacts and professional references to provide background information. It is, in many ways your freeway billboard—you are the product you are selling. The one big drawback of a resume is that once you send it out, it may be in circulation for many years; if it is poorly written, you may miss out on several coveted positions without knowing it.

What the Resume Isn't

Many people write their resume in lieu of an autobiography. It is not meant to be an autobiography of your accomplishments. It is meant to create interest on the employer's part and demonstrate your capacity to solve the employer's problems. Understand that candidates are hired to solve problems. The details and facts listed on your resume support your experience in solving problems, but it's not your personal history. While it may be your job history, it can still be written in a way that creates interest. If you write with that goal in mind, your final product will be very different than if you just present your job history. Show some enthusiasm and create a masterpiece. If you can't do it yourself, hire someone to do it for you.

Your Resume

Before you create your resume, you will need to decide what effect you want it to have on the reader. Anticipating the reader's reaction has to play the key role in its design. And yes, you *will* need to design a separate resume for each position or business sector or tweak the resume to fit. I am often surprised to receive resumes for position X that were clearly written for position Y and sent to me for interpretation. On one occasion, I received a call from an individual inquiring about the status of his resume. I welcomed the opportunity to ask what the individual was thinking when he decided to submit an ill-fitting resume for the position. Sometimes I learn the candidate felt some remotely similar activity met the requirements. Sadly, most of the time, the answer is a patent demonstration of laziness or superiority (or a combination of both): the individual was too busy to tailor the resume because of the challenges of his current position.

There is no right or wrong way to write a resume. Recognize that competition for jobs is fierce and your resume must set you apart from the masses. In order for your resume to land you an interview, from which you must land the job, it must be a passionate representation of who you are and why you are the best person for the job.

Don't be afraid to delineate the benefits of hiring you over someone else. Organizations need to know that you will help them attain their corporate objectives. Your resume is your best chance to prove that capability. Not one resume in a hundred follows the principles that stir the interest of prospective employers. Even if the competition is fierce, a well-written resume should garner invitations to interview more often and give you a leg up on many people more qualified than you.

To understand what I mean, consider the purpose of your resume. Why do you have a resume in the first place? What is it supposed to do for you? You send your resume with a cover letter to the prospective employer. Understand, there may be one hundred other candidates who feel the same way you do. They, too, are perfect for the same job. In a matter of days, the employer has 101 resumes to review. The number of resumes being sent in desperation (this is, after all, a down economy) will far exceed this conservative estimate of only one hundred resumes. I have many times received more than five hundred resumes for a single position that was posted on a single Web site.

Reviewing resumes is a task, not a pleasure. The reviewer, faced with a mountain of resumes, quickly loses enthusiasm and focus. That number I mentioned earlier, sixty seconds to review a resume, drops exponentially as the reviewer tries to reduce the pile of would-be candidates. Reviewers have a picture in mind of the perfect resume; if it comes up, it is quickly put in the contact file. These lucky people will be called or invited to interview. The other resumes are filed away or discarded.

6. The Resume in Detail

The Four Resume Styles

Always listen to experts. They'll tell you what can't be done and why. Then do it.

—Robert Heinlein

There are four styles of resumes: chronological, functional, combination, and narrative.

Chronological Style

The overwhelming favorite of candidates and employers alike is the chronological resume, a classic style providing a wealth of information in a format that is both easy to skim and digest. The chronological resume lists the candidate's jobs in reverse chronological order, with the accomplishments and activities of each job clearly identified by particular company, title, and tenure. The reader has some confidence that there is someone at every company listed who can verify each and every claim.

In current practice executive/professional-level chronological resumes frequently begin with a brief profile summarizing a candidate's talents, series of accomplishments, or highlights of past successes. Using any or all of these stylistic techniques, the

24

most pertinent information can be presented in the first few lines of the resume. The modern chronological resume places the most important information at the top of the resume, with the more extensive and detailed career data at the bottom. It has a high verifiability factor, giving the reader confidence in the document. When properly designed, it is easy to skim quickly.

Most employers prefer chronological resumes because the applicant's career progression is readily discernible. Most of the advice and recommendations provided here relate most closely with the chronological format. This style combines the primary elements of the chronological and functional resume formats by presenting relevant skills and abilities, but in chronological order. Because many reviewers read resumes from bottom to top to evaluate the logical career pattern or lack thereof, a chronological-style resume is best suited to this task.

The chronological resume is the most traditional structure for a resume. The Experience section should be the focus; each job (or the last several jobs) is described in some detail, and though the Experience section may be preceded by a few lines summarizing skills or accomplishments for executive/professional-level jobs, there is no major section of skills or accomplishments at the beginning of the resume. This structure is primarily used by those who remain in the same profession or same type of work, particularly in very conservative fields. It is also favored in law and academia. It is widely recommended that the chronological resume always have an Objective or Summary, to focus the reader.

The advantage of a chronological-style resume is that it may appeal to older, more traditional readers and be best suited to very conservative fields, such as banking and finance. Its structure makes it easier to understand what you did in what job. The disadvantage is that it is much more difficult to highlight what you do best. This format is rarely appropriate for someone looking to make a career change.

Functional Style

The functional-style resume presents experience and/or skills claims from all jobs under topical headings, such as "finance," "marketing," or "management," and usually includes a separate section where the jobs are simply listed (company and title) in reverse chronological order, dates optional. The problem with this style is that it is hard to tie a specific claim of accomplishment to a particular job. The proper context is obscured and it is difficult to verify the statements being made.

This style is a favorite with candidates who have something to hide, and for that reason it is far more popular with candidates than with employers. For example, in a functional resume, there might be a note under the management heading, "Managed a team of ten," and in the job chronology, there might be a note about being in a vice president role. The reasonable (and desired, on the part of the candidate) assumption is that the candidate managed this team of ten people as the vice president, whereas the reality might be that the candidate has not worked as a vice president in over a year and the team may have been managed under another position in a much lesser role.

Because the functional resume concentrates on skills and abilities, it is only a benefit to job-hoppers and individuals returning to the work force. Names of employers, dates of employment, and education history details are omitted and the information is not presented chronologically. The functional resume is the least effective for landing interviews, let alone job offers, because it is meant to tease the reader into pursuing the candidate for more information. In most cases, this will not happen. Interviewers are far too busy to waste time with teasers and posers.

Combination Style

Like a garbage pizza that offers the consumer some of everything, a combination-style resume includes elements of both the chronological and functional formats. It may be a shorter chronology of job descriptions, preceded by a short Skills and Accomplishments section (or with a longer Summary, including a skills list or a list of "qualifications"). Alternatively, it may be a standard functional resume with the accomplishments under headings of different jobs held.

There are obvious advantages to this combined approach: It maximizes the advantages of both kinds of resumes, avoiding potential negative effects of either type. One disadvantage is that it tends to be a longer resume, but in today's employment market, that may not be a problem. Another negative is that it can be repetitious: Accomplishments and skills may have to be repeated in both the "functional" section and the "chronological" job descriptions; this may not be a bad thing, in that an electronic keyword search would identify more "hits" on this resume.

Narrative Style

The narrative-style resume is a third-person promotional piece. It is a common feature of business proposals and marketing materials. It can be written about either an individual or company. When the subject is an individual, the profile can focus on the career or be fully biographical in scope. The narrative format makes it easy to obscure any unpleasant details. The narrative resume is not common to the job-search arena. Narrative resumes seem to come most often from the design and creativity areas, where seeing the big picture (vision) is deemed more important than the details of what was accomplished.

Appearance

Select a design and format that allows you to highlight the information about your work experience, skills, and education that is the most directly relevant to the job for which you are applying. Keep the layout clean and easy to read to help pull the reader in. There was a time when the paper resume was king, but that time has passed. Today, few companies will accept a paper resume because it requires an extra processing step to scan that paper resume into the resume database.

When sending an e-mail resume, *do not* aspire to greatness by laying out your resume in a fancy format using Photoshop.

Remember, your objective is not to entertain but to get the recruiters to "welcome" your resume into their database. Many databases don't support unique files. *Never* put your contact information in the header of your resume. Search firms' software can't get to it there. Two things to *always* do: paste the resume in the body of the e-mail message itself and attach a copy. The pasted copy can be reviewed quickly (by a human) and the attached copy can be easily forwarded to hiring managers or placed in the resume database.

The first level of resume prescreening via the Internet is done on a keyword basis. You will increase the chances of your resume being searched and reviewed by potential employers if you incorporate keywords and phrases that describe core skills required for the type of job you are seeking. Also, be sure to keep your resume updated and consistent across all of the sites you decide to use.

Make sure, if you are using Web sites to distribute your resume, that you get it sent to yourself to check the ease of downloading it. Some sites add so much promotional material to your resume page that it's impossible to download the resume to a retrieval system. To ensure the resume will make it into a resume retrieval system, attach it to an e-mail message sent directly to the company of interest.

Resumes should begin with your name, street address, e-mail address, and phone number(s). Make it easy for a potential employer to contact you. Avoid including personal information such as a picture, age, height, weight, or marital status; it is both unnecessary and out of place. Never use colored paper, watermarks, or designs of any type. While they might catch attention of the reviewer, it won't be the kind of attention you want and they do not scan well. "Pretty" resumes and "fancy" resumes both end up in the trash.

Not long ago, I would have advised keeping your resume to two pages at the most. Well, times have changed and competition is now a factor. Today, I would advise stretching the resume to three and if the experience merits, four pages in length. The change from two pages to a longer resume may separate you from the pack and result in a perceived depth of experience. A well-summarized representation of your work history, experience, and education has a much bigger impact than a narrative that details every position you have ever held.

Grammar and Punctuation

A mistake in grammar or punctuation always catches the eye of a reviewer and, in most cases, ends the review. Unfortunately, there is a tendency for reviewers to look for ways to screen out candidates rather than to screen in candidates. A mistake in grammar or punctuation says you did not take the time to get it right and that may be how you would perform in a position. It calls to attention your lack of attention to detail. Interestingly, salespeople normally have these types of mistakes because they are focused on closing the sale, not the details of the deal. A perfect resume from a salesperson might indicate an individual who is so focused on the details that deals are missed and not closed. It's a balancing act, but it's best to err on the side of perfection.

The Parts of a Resume

Your Profile

Opening your resume with a brief profile is a great way to make a resume powerful. Some people say it's not important, but it's the first thing the reviewer sees, unless the reviewer is screening out by residence. Properly written, a profile will generate the interest to get your resume read and not merely skimmed. Sometimes it takes longer to write the profile than the resume.

The better you understand the position you are applying for, the more precise you can be in writing your profile. Though the profile is critical, don't make the mistake of making it too long; it has to be brief to have impact, no more than three to five sentences in length. Even if you are a little vague about what you are looking for, you cannot let your uncertainty show. A nonexistent, vague, or overly broad profile is worse than no profile at all; it says you are not sure this is the job for you. If the job is right for you, your profile needs to say why. Here's an example of a good profile:

> *Profile/Expertise—An accomplished software sales professional who has mastered selling Oracle applications with an extraordinary record of generating new accounts, consistently exceeding sales targets and providing enthusiastic customer relations.*

This sort of profile wakes up the reader and generates immediate interest. This first sentence conveys some very important and powerful messages: "I want the exact job you are offering. I am a superior candidate because I recognize the qualities that are most important to you, and I have them. I want to make a contribution to your company." This profile works well because the employer is smart enough to know that someone who wants to do exactly what they are offering will be much more likely to succeed than someone who doesn't. As a bonus, that person will probably be a lot more pleasant to work with.

Secondly, this candidate has done a good job of establishing in the very first sentence why he or she is the perfect candidate. He or she has thought about what qualities would make a candidate stand out and has communicated the matches. What's more, the skills and assets are communicated from the point of view of making a contribution to the employer.

This candidate recognized that the prospective employer, being a small, growing software company, would be very interested in candidates with an ability to generate new accounts. Having intuited that important fact, the candidate made that the very first point to get communicated in the resume. Make the most of those few seconds of attention your resume might receive. Start by generating interest with a powerful, laser-focused profile.

If you are applying for several different positions, you should adapt your profile and resume to each one. There is nothing wrong with having several different resumes, each with a different profile objective, each specifically crafted for a different type of position. You may even want to change some parts of your resume for each job you apply for. Your profile should match the job you are applying for. Remember, you are writing a marketing elevator pitch (a rehearsed presentation), not your life story.

If you are making a career change or have a limited work history, you want the employer to focus immediately on where you are going, rather than where you have or have not been. If you are looking for another job in your present field, it is more important to stress your qualities, achievements, and abilities first.

Ideally, your resume should be steered toward conveying why you are the perfect candidate for one specific job or job title. Good advertising is targeted to a very specific market or audience. Your profile can and should be targeted for different types of positions. Targeting your profile requires you to be absolutely clear—or at least that you appear to be clear—about your career direction. Whether you have a job or are out of work, there is no better time than the present to chart the path of your future career so you have a clear target that will meet your goals and be personally fulfilling.

Experience

Under the Experience section of your resume, list your employers, starting with your current employer, job locations, employment dates, job titles, and descriptions of your tasks, accomplishments, and skills. Employers want to know what you did and how closely that experience matches their needs. Include only the most important information about each position. Be sure to include a list of key contributions or achievements in every position. Rather than list fifteen bulleted items, list six or seven of the most important. When reviewers see a laundry list of accomplishments, their first reaction is to assume it is filler meant to impress. Be specific rather than general in your descriptions. Use concise, vivid language. Quantify the impact of your actions in your previous positions. Facts, figures, and numbers help to do this. For example, how many accounts did you work on? How many employees did you supervise? How much revenue did you generate?

List jobs in reverse chronological order, but don't detail the jobs early in your career. Focus on the most recent and/or relevant jobs. (Summarize a number of the earliest jobs in one line or very short paragraph, or list only the bare facts with no position description.) Decide which, overall, is more impressive—your job titles or the names of the firms you worked for—then consistently begin with the more impressive of the two. Put dates in italics at the end of the job, to de-emphasize them; don't include months, unless the job was held less than a year.

Education

Education statements should include dates of attendance, majors, minors, and degrees. List your most recent or impressive educational achievement first. Include additional coursework if it is related to the position in question. List unique talents or specialized skills in hot demand in your field of interest in this section as well.

Awards

Whether to include awards is a subject of great debate. Listing awards not related to the job of interest doesn't enhance your candidacy and detracts from the meat of your resume. On the other hand, awards that recognize your accomplishments, skill, or leadership—awards that indicate others think you are special—could be worth including.

Your Target

If you are searching for a job but are not sure you are on a career path that is right for you, chances are you will jump for an opportunity for which you are probably ill fitted and that doesn't suit your personal or professional needs. If you take such a job, you will probably find it unfulfilling and most likely will leave the position within a few months or years.

Research shows that only one interview is granted for every 245 resumes received by the average employer. Research also tells us that your resume will be quickly scanned. What this means is that the decision to interview a candidate is usually based on an overall first impression of the resume, a quick screening that so impresses the reader and convinces them of the candidate's qualifications that an interview results. For this reason, the Profile section of your resume will either make you or break you. By the time the first few lines of your resume are scanned, you have either caught the reader's interest or your resume has failed. That is why we say that your resume is a marketing piece.

To write a marketing resume, you have to master the "elevator pitch." Not only that, but you must sell yourself as the product. What's worse, given the fact that most of us do not think along the lines of marketing, you are probably not looking forward to selling anything, let alone yourself. But if you want to increase your job-hunting effectiveness, you would be wise to learn to write a spectacular resume. Do some research on marketing pitches to get some creative ideas. There are a lot of marketing books available that have some great examples you can adopt.

There is no need for hard-selling yourself. You can make a point without hitting the reader over the head. Absolutely do not make any claims that aren't 100 percent true. That said, this is not the time to be shy about your abilities. If you don't promote yourself, who will? Employers like to be sold and more often buy the best-marketed product. With a little extra effort, you will usually get a better response from prospective employers. Imagine that you are the person doing the hiring. This person is not some anonymous human resources person but someone who screens resumes as part of his or her job. He or she is an expert in identifying and acquiring talent. If you are seeking a job in a field you know well, you probably already know what would make someone a superior candidate. If you are not addressing those real needs, no employer will respond to your resume.

There are two parts to a resume. In the first part, you assert your abilities, qualities, and achievements in a powerful marketing pitch—the Profile—that makes the reader immediately perk up and realize that you are someone special. In the second part, you reinforce your assertions with evidence—Experience—that you actually did what you said you did.

Resume Problems

Positions Held

Generally, it is reasonable to go back five to ten years in your work history. If your work history is lengthier than that, you may want to disclose only the last ten years of experience. It's not being dishonest to leave out past experience that does not help support your current career. If an interviewer asks you about past positions, address each one in general terms and identify briefly what you accomplished. Reviewers do not expect or want your life history.

Work Gaps

Rather than leave a gap, it is best to indicate what you were doing: whether you were a full-time parent, on maternity leave, traveling, studying, or volunteering. If you are currently in a work gap, you may want to consider fitting in some volunteer work along with the job search. This ancillary sort of work is an excellent element to include in your resume. It shows you have some initiative and, if your volunteer work supports an organization or cause favored by the potential employer, it'll catch the reviewer's eye.

Job Hopping

Job hopping produces more red flags than a May Day parade in Moscow. If your resume lists many positions, each of which was held for a short period of time (from one to two years or less), despite the best of reasons or excuses (e.g., merger, downsizing, company gone out of business), chances are you will not be viewed in a positive light.

If possible, consider redrafting your resume format to exclude as many short-term positions as possible, indicating only the ones with a longer tenure, *or* exclude all dates on your resume. Some reviewers may toss a resume that has no dates, but there are those who may see the experience and the scope of responsibilities held in a positive light and call you to inquire as to why you didn't add dates. You will have achieved the first objective—getting a recruiter/employer to call you. Once you have engaged the recruiter or employer in friendly (but not too friendly) discussion on the phone, you can discuss your rationale for these repeated job changes in a positive manner, hopefully meriting a face-to-face interview. As an executive recruiter, I have called and met with many candidates who did not list dates on their resumes for this very reason; I have moved forward with some of them as candidates, comfortable explaining to my clients the circumstances surrounding their many positions.

Criminal Past

A criminal past is hard to overcome. There is no good way to package past bad behavior that will make it acceptable to most risk-adverse employers. Trying to hide the past is impossible; everyone has Internet access and everything's available on the Internet. A simple background check will reveal everything from criminal records to credit problems and driving accidents. Employers are required to protect themselves, their employees, and their shareholders. Knowing they can be held liable if an employee commits an unlawful act and it is determined the employee was not vetted before being hired, employers' needs for full disclosure are understandable.

Even if you're not a criminal, crime can still affect your employment options. For instance, some states allow employers to dismiss domestic violence victims who are at-will employees; they dismiss them under the guise of presenting or creating a risk to coworkers.

If you're unsure about what an employer will check, ask. The more you know, the better you can prepare yourself with a suitable explanation. Check with the state you're in as to the rules and regulations that impact your employment.

The best advice is to always tell the truth when faced with a question concerning your background. Being caught in a lie will *always* result in rejection or immediate dismissal, whereas being honest often gives you the opportunity to explain the situation, resulting in a more positive decision.

If you have a checkered past, the best advice might be to target your job search on small employers who may not delve too deeply into your background.

Embellishment

Mistakes happen. Messing up a starting or ending date of employment can be overlooked by a recruiter, but embellishments of achievements and accomplishments, when discovered in the interviewing process, reflect negatively on the individual's honesty and character. Many candidates embellish a bit when describing their experiences, accomplishments, and achievements, just as companies embellish when they tell you how wonderful they and their career opportunities are.

You transcend (or should I say descend) from embellishment to misrepresentation when you stretch the facts beyond credibility, such as when you make up degrees or positions. One popular area on a resume that seems to attract embellishment is Education. Candidates always want to present themselves as highly educated; they push the limits to rise above their competitors. The first resume "fact" that any self-respecting employer or recruiter verifies is a person's education. Many companies do this quick and easy check before they even pick up the phone to chat with you or consider scheduling an interview. Don't embellish your education.

Resume Mistakes

Overconfidence can hurt your chances for success. If you start out with the mindset that says, "they need me; I will send an overview of my accomplishments," or send a multi-page resume covering several decades of your career, you will be surprised by the number of calls and invitations to interview that you *don't* receive. When I receive an overview resume, I throw it away. I really don't have the time to contact the candidate and beg for more information; no recruiter or employer will waste time with that candidate, because that candidate hasn't taken the time to understand and appreciate the employer's needs. The multi-page resume gets a quick one or two page review. I am only interested in what the candidate did in the last ten years. If the candidate is applying for a position and the related experience was gained more than ten years ago, the candidacy is not viable. It's brutal, but it's business.

Focusing on years of experience rather than on accomplishments is another common mistake. It telegraphs to the recruiter or employer that you have done the same thing over and over again throughout your career; you have a comfort zone and cannot operate beyond it. Instead, a focus on accomplishments demonstrates depth of experience, flexibility, and confidence to move from one challenging assignment to another. It goes without saying, but let me say it anyway; these accomplishments should be related to problem solving, not personal matters.

Reapplying for a Job

Unless you are applying for a different position with an employer that you have applied to in the past, and you meet all the requirements, you may be wasting your time. Companies today have resume systems that keep track of every time you have applied for a position. When a recruiter opens up your resume in the system, he or she sees that you have applied and been rejected before. If you apply for all types of positions, your resume will be flagged (in a bad way) and rejected upon submission. Many resume systems automatically flag (in a good way) your resume for any position that matches your skills and notify you, the recruiter, or the employer. This means that reapplying for a job or applying for many jobs at the same company reflects desperation. Recruiters and employers don't want to work with desperate candidates.

7. Letters of Introduction (Cover Letters)

You have to be original. If you're like everyone else, what do they need you for?

—*B. Peters*

Most cover letters are a waste of time. They all say the same things, so recruiters and employers spend little time reading them. I know, you've heard other experts harp on its importance in concert with your resume, but usually only the resume is reviewed and placed in the resume retrieval system; your cover letter gets you an X in the checklist and then gets chucked in the trash. I concur a cover letter is useful if you have something of importance to say in it, such as "Mary Johnson, Senior Vice President of Marketing at Zoolo Corporation, who considers you one of the top marketing professionals in the software industry, asked me to contact you directly. I am a marketing professional, and Mary felt I could be an asset to your marketing group. Mary also asked for you to contact her directly if you needed additional background information." Now, a statement like this one will catch the eye of any recruiter/hiring manager and possibly generate a phone call, with either you or Mary to follow up on your resume. Be sure you have Mary's permission before you drop her name and invite someone to call her.

This is an example of a real cover letter that commits some common mistakes:

Good afternoon.

I understand that your firm frequently conducts searches for outstanding corporate executives. My objective is to find a position that will put my experience to the best possible use, while adding significant value to an organization.

I am open to exploring career opportunities in any field, but I am particularly interested in companies that are in growth sectors of the IT and global communications marketplace. I have enclosed a copy of my resume that will give you a summary of my background and accomplishments as well as a feel for the diverse responsibilities I have enjoyed as a CEO, Sales and Marketing Executive, and Corporate Strategist.

Should any of your current assignments call for a high-energy, innovative and entrepreneurial leader with a proven track record in fast-paced environments, please contact me at the number listed on my resume.

I would be happy to speak with you to review my background and qualifications in more detail, and look forward to hearing from you in the near future.

Sincerely,

A cover letter should be addressed to a specific person if possible. It should also open with a comment that grabs the reader's attention in order to have impact. When writing an unsolicited letter, it helps to say someone requested your resume; if possible, mention the name of someone you may know in the company. If contacting an executive search firm, do not state in the cover letter that you have researched the search firm if you haven't. For example, if you say you understand the search firm has an excellent record for placing medical professionals, and the firm does not recruit in the health care sector, this makes you look unprepared or downright careless and your resume ends up in the trash. Stating that you were referred to the recruiter or firm by someone unknown to the firm is also a no-no. A quick check of the database tells the recruiter if this individual is a client, candidate, or unknown to the firm. Trying to start a relationship with a small lie is a non-starter.

What Must the Letter Achieve?

A cover letter is basically your second piece of marketing material. Your first is the resume. You are trying to inspire a specific action—an invitation for a phone interview that will lead to a face-to-face interview. In addition to reinforcing the key skills and experience referenced in your resume, a cover letter provides the opportunity to:

- Demonstrate your interest in working for the employer
- Identify specific ways your expertise can benefit the organization
- Differentiate yourself from other job seekers
- Explain anomalies that may stand out in a resume, such as job changes in employment

What Do You Offer?

Each cover letter you send should be customized for each individual employer and include a statement about why you are attracted to the position and company. If you send a generic letter, you will be lucky to get any reaction at all.

Before you begin writing your letter, learn as much as you can about the potential employer/recruiter. The more you know about an organization, the better you can tailor your cover letter to the firm's needs. Visit the firm's Web site and scan industry publications so you are up to speed on recent news about the company.

Remember, you want to express what you can do for the employer/recruiter, not what they can do for you. A cover letter must highlight aspects of your experience that are most useful to the potential employer.

Make It Personal

Job listings rarely include the name of the hiring manager/ recruiter. Never begin a cover letter with "To whom it may concern" or "Dear hiring manager." A generic salutation signals to potential employers and recruiters that you lack the initiative to locate the appropriate contact. Instead, call the company directly and explain the position you are applying for to see if you can fill in the blank with a person's name. Alternatively, take time to research on the Internet or in appropriate business periodicals to get the name and title of the hiring official. Another good place to look is the firm's financial statements, which often include organizational charts.

A Professional Presentation

A good cover letter begins with a powerful, clearly written opening paragraph. Your goal is to briefly describe how you heard about the position and why you're interested in it. If you're replying to a published opening, refer to this in your cover letter as well as any information specifically requested. Your tone should be confident. Avoid gimmicky attempts to gain attention; they are often perceived as insincere. It is best to keep your letter polished and professional as well as interesting and visually appealing. Mention only positive things and be formal.

What Is Relevant?

A cover letter should be brief and to the point. It should be no longer than one page—perhaps three or four paragraphs. Recruiters are busy people and often only have time to skim through applications. Use statistics, highlighted statements, or bullets to make sure that vital information can be spotted easily and quickly. Make sure the message in your letter is consistent with the information included in your resume. Your cover letter should not be a laundry list of items from your resume. Instead, highlight skills and experiences that are most relevant to the job opening and provide concrete examples of the skills, training, and/or experiences that are the basis for your confidence.

Grammar and Spelling Errors Will Kill Your Chances

The smallest grammatical error on your part can call your professionalism and attention to detail into question, thereby discouraging a hiring manager from contacting you for an interview. *Always* spell-check your document before sending it to any potential employer. Spell-checking will likely pick up words that are misspelled, but will not necessarily pick up incorrect words, such as those that sound alike but are wrong in context. *They're*, *their*, and *there* are all spelled correctly, but they are not interchangeable. Be sure to proofread for word accuracy as well as spelling and grammar. If you are not confident of your skills in this area, find someone to help you.

Following Up

In addition to expressing gratitude for the hiring manager's time and interest, close your letter by outlining your next steps. Be proactive. State when you will contact him or her to follow up. Don't forget to include a phone number and e-mail address where you can be reached in case the firm wants to get in touch with you first. I suggest making your first contact by e-mail and not by phone call because e-mail messages are much less intrusive and can be responded to at the convenience of the recipient.

Be sure to follow up with the employer via e-mail in two to three weeks if you have not received a response. In your follow up e-mail, reiterate your interest in the position, ask about the status of your application, and ask if any further information is needed from you to help the employer reach a decision regarding who will be interviewed.

8. Who Do You Know?

Networking

It's not what you know but who you know that makes the difference.

—Unknown

The best method for finding a new position involves personal networking. Take inventory of all your contacts, and then arrange them in priority order of importance. As you compile your list, be realistic. Ask yourself whether the contact is someone who is at a level sufficient to really help you in your search. If the answer is yes, then let your contacts know you are looking for a position. Don't forget to ask them for their career input and advice.

While you might think all your old friends could be good networking contacts, think again. Choose for your job search contacts network those individuals who have the influence and business contacts that can actually help your career, and not just your morale. Concentrate on making connections with individuals and their contacts at the highest levels in an organization, because they will have the most influence over or know of positions you seek. Mid-level managers and human resources professionals who do not have the visibility or responsibility over positions may be good second-tier connections. Contacts in professional areas or industries outside of your career focus are, for the most part, a waste of time.

When pulling together a contact list, consider how and how well the individual (e.g., coworker, manager, client, or vendor) knows you and your accomplishments. It is assumed you will choose individuals who are or were impressed with your performance on the job; if you are unsure about their "take" on you, do not include them on your list. You need to rely on the contact to assist you, not undermine you.

An old and worthwhile trick to use when making a contact (if you know the contact well) is to ask the individual to be a reference for you in your job search rather than asking for a job, since the individual knows you well. This relieves some of the pressure on the contact, because he or she will not be on the spot to create or find a job for you; often relieving someone of this sort of pressure makes them want to help you more, which may generate an opportunity anyway.

Never end a call to a contact without asking for additional referrals of new contacts he or she may have thought of for you. The down side of personal networking is that the chances of someone knowing of a possible position are low. It may be too late to build a successful personal network before you actually need to use it, but if you don't start now, you'll never have one. Respond with enthusiasm when asked to assist someone else who is networking. Also, keep circling back to contacts to report on your progress; this will serve as a gentle reminder of your interest in their help and may expand their value. On the other hand, don't be a pest. Their job is not to find you a job. Personal networks tend to not be very successful if you fail to follow up.

Beware of overaggressive networking. Sometimes a contact claims he or she knows an important person and you phone that individual, mention your contact's name, and get rebuffed. What happened? The simple truth is no one wants to have their time wasted by someone referred by someone known only casually, if at all. If your contact claims to know the person, ask your contact to arrange a brief conversation for you. If you're all in the same geographic locale, make it a face-to-face meeting. If you're not geographically proximate, make it a phone conversation. If your contact isn't willing or able to arrange a meeting or phone conversation for you, then maybe your contact doesn't have the relationship he or she told you existed.

When you phone a contact or someone recommended by a contact, listen carefully to the tone of voice. You will know quickly if this call is of value or if this person is in a position to help you and is willing to do so. Get to the point; be concise and don't waste anyone's time trying to make a new friend. See if you get the feeling the person on the other end of the phone is willing and able to help you try to get a face-to-face meeting with the individual. If this isn't possible—and there is a high probability that it will not happen—welcome any advice offered over the phone.

Understand, executives receive many such calls and dislike being pressured into the situation. I had at least three calls a week in my executive roles. At first, I accepted the invitation to meet for fifteen minutes, which always dragged into double the time or more. I disliked these meetings because, most times, there was nothing I could offer the individual but my impression of them selling their background and experience. I stopped meeting or speaking with any referral unless I had confirmed the quality of the individual with whomever had referred him or her to me. If I was convinced of the caliber of the individual, I accepted the contact and followed up with the referrer on my impressions, to make sure we both understood the needs of the organization and the use of my time.

Another factor in making this decision involved how the initial contact was made and the impression I got during that contact. If the contact was by phone, I listened for the energy level in the person's voice, the clarity of the message being communicated, and the specific career path of interest. If the career path was outside my area of expertise, a conversation with the individual would waste both of our time, as well as my possible referral contacts.

Getting to Decision Makers

The critical ingredient is getting off your butt and doing something. It's as simple as that. A lot of people have ideas, but there are few who decide to do something about them now. Not tomorrow. Not next week. But today, the true entrepreneur is a doer.

—Nolan Bushnell

Many experts will tell you not to go around the system (the HR department) in your job search. I disagree. Staffing needs are often discussed at the hiring managers' level long before a requisition is approved and given to HR to start the recruiting process. Every organization has individuals in line for promotion or poor performers in line for the door, but a replacement needs to be found before the organization can take action on that individual. Promotions and dismissals happen in both good and bad times.

By design, senior-level managers are insulated from the outside world. They will not accept a call without knowing the caller and the subject of the call, and most have their e-mails screened. Most senior-level managers do not want to be bothered or distracted by individuals seeking a job; that's why organizations have HR departments.

Given this understanding, why bother trying to circumvent the HR department? Consider and make use of all possible avenues in your job search process. Getting your resume in the hands of the right manager at the right time may expedite your search process. Put yourself in a manager's position: You have a need but you are too busy to get around to getting a requisition pulled together, and finding the right person might involve kissing a lot of frogs first.

Imagine, then, receiving the perfect resume from outside the organization. A solution fell into your lap. No frogs. You contact the candidate and discuss the position. A lot of executives enjoy sticking it to the HR people by finding the perfect candidate when the HR people claim they can't. The candidate fits the position; you then contact the HR people, present them with the candidate's resume, and bring in the candidate for the interview. If this sounds farfetched, I'm here to tell you it's not. This happens more often than you know. The objective, after all, is to solve a problem. When the right individual presents himself or herself, the problem is solved. Yes, you will experience some resentment from the HR people, but if the fit is there, you will have a new position, HR will take the credit for filling the position, and pretty soon after you're on board, nobody will remember the circumstances under which you arrived.

The strategy of how to "get to the decision makers" involves first doing an honest assessment of your abilities, skills, and experience. By these attributes, I mean what you can contribute quickly to a new position, not what you feel you might be able to do.

Research the companies that are a match for your abilities and target the executive who is responsible for the area where you expertise would be of value. Popular options are marketing, sales, engineering, finance, and operations. With some diligence on your part, you should be able to find the current senior managers, as well as the 10K (Public Company Report) on every company in which you have even a passing interest. A company's 10K will provide a wealth of information on the issues the organization may be facing, giving you the items to stress in the resume and cover letter you use to present yourself to the senior manager.

Start with Web sites like LinkedIn to see if any high-level executives are listed. Even if they are not in the targeted area of the company, consider sending them your resume and ask if they would pass it on to the manager of the department, group, or division that interests you. You might be surprised; sometimes they do.

Since your resume, if sent in directly to your desired contact, has a high probability of being redirected to human resources by the administrative assistant who screens the hiring manager's e-mail, this is not the best approach to gain that individual's attention.

Absent a powerful referral/endorsement from an individual who knows the possible hiring manager, the best way to get the manager's attention is a well-written cover letter and resume targeting a possible problem or issue facing the manager that you can help resolve. Have it delivered marked personal and confidential by FedEx. Most administrative assistants will not open materials marked personal and confidential.

I have heard of instances in which a direct approach to the division executive or even the president of the company has been effective and can have some impact in getting someone in the organization interested in your background. The key is what you can do for them that no one else can do. This information has to come through strongly in your written presentation. Be aware that using this approach after you've been shot down by the hiring manager is a bad idea, because that manager might feel pressured to hire you if the request is made from above. Nobody likes to feel pressured into doing something he or she might otherwise not do.

The downside of going directly to the hiring manager or higher, rather than through the HR department, is you may receive a rejection letter, which you might have received anyway, even if you had played by the rules. If you are unique, then *be* unique. Bold leaders go directly to the decision makers, rather than wait by the phone hoping for a date to the prom.

9. Agencies/Search Firms

Search Firms

We judge ourselves by what we feel capable of doing, while others judge us by what we have already done.

—Henry Wadsworth Longfellow

Do I really need to say it? Yes, I think I do. Use some common sense when contacting executive recruiters. All search firms receive letters and calls from candidates pushing their candidacy for positions. Many candidates mention their willingness to help source other candidates for the recruiter using their Rolodex or electronic address book of business contacts. The reason for offering this is to get the opportunity to speak with the recruiter and subliminally sell themselves while being of assistance. I doubt there exists an "I want to be of assistance" approach that hasn't been tried on an executive recruiter in one form or another.

If you have the ability to influence an organization (in other words, you are a key player), then state in your contact letter to executive recruiters that, if the recruiter is successful in placing you in the right position, you will do your best to expand the recruiters' influence and continue placements within the organization. Executive recruiters are always focused on building their business and the easiest way to accomplish this is to increase business with a known client. When I read this statement in an

49

introduction letter, I pay attention to the candidate's ability to actually deliver future business to my firm. If the candidate is at the right level with the right experience, he or she has my attention.

There is no risk in this approach for you the candidate, because if the recruiter does a professional job in placing you with an organization, you know the quality and abilities of the recruiter, and the recruiter understands you and your expectations. You have worked well together and can expect the positive relationship you have established to continue.

Along with networking with everyone who may be of value to you in your job search, a necessary source to activate is the executive search community. The level of position you are seeking helps to define the type of search company that should be contacted and made aware of your availability.

People ask me all the time how search firms work. The answer is simple. Using today's technology, anyone with research experience can target any company and source candidates. Search firms employ trained staffs who compile candidate contacts for future search needs. Most search firms receive hundreds of resumes from individuals wanting to be noticed. Databases expand in the normal course of collecting resumes and conducting searches. In addition, past candidates continue to refer new candidates in order to have a continued presence on the search professional's radar screen.

As standard operating procedure, search firms maintain thousands of contacts, all just a few keyboard clicks away, so they can quickly identify and promote possible candidates for any given position. One method of sourcing candidates is to send broadcast e-mails with sourcing specifications to all the contacts in the database and ask for any possible referrals. Timing is one of the most important and underrated aspects of recruiting. It can take three to eight months to find a suitable candidate.

Every successful recruiting effort starts with an understanding of what is required by the client in terms of years of experience, particular skills, and personality fit. Executive search consultants draw on their experience conducting similar searches, but because every organization is different, every organization's staffing needs are also different. The search consultant's role is to gather the requirements and formulate the information into a concise position description and get agreement before initiating a search. This is the first step in the search process on the client side of the transaction. Since the client/consultant relationship is a fairly intimate one, openness and honesty in the exchange of ideas is essential. Hidden agendas cause problems and delay progress. The consultant has the task of determining, based on the requirements, whether the candidate sought really exists and would accept the position if it were offered as structured. If not, it's back to the drawing board.

The two types of executive search firms are retained and contingency. Retained search firms are hired by companies to find candidates for their higher-level positions. Normally, they only work to fill positions at the $150,000 and up levels: the directors, vice presidents, executive vice presidents, and CEOs. Retained firms get paid by the company even if a candidate is not found. They have a guaranteed fee structure. The fact that they rarely miss placing a candidate and guarantee the performance of the candidate is why they can command their high fees. Retained firms take a rifle shot approach (as opposed to a shotgun approach) to placing candidates. Retained search firms can be difficult to deal with as a candidate, unless you have expertise that is needed in their client's business sector.

Contingency search firms service both upper-level and mid-management positions. Contingency firms take on assignments for companies with no money up front. They can only collect a fee if their candidate is hired by the company, which is part of the reason why contingency firms use a shotgun approach to placement. They send out a large number of unsolicited resumes in the hope of getting a company interested in seeing their candidate. Contingency search firms normally appreciate receiving your resume because of their style of promoting candidates; the more candidates they have to promote, the better their chances of landing a fee.

When working with a search firm, you will need to develop a bond of trust with the consultant. This part of the process involves getting to know you better to assess your potential and placement probability. Although the relationship is close, it is not exclusive. Consultants deal with multiple candidates and searches

51

at the same time. The consultant should show you respect, but you must recognize you are, essentially, a commodity. If you, the commodity, are properly handled and placed, you will solve a client's problem and enrich the consultant. Clients often demand a slate of candidates—sometimes five to ten—to be submitted all at once before they'll review any of the resumes and schedule interviews. This process takes time to complete when you consider the time required to vet a single candidate.

The consultant has to keep the candidates happy in order to complete the process. The slate of candidates process is, in some ways, very straightforward: You put your top candidate in the middle of a slate, because 75 percent of the time, hiring managers select the candidate in the middle. This is similar to the approach often recommended with multiple-choice questions; when in doubt, choose C. The slate of candidates is assembled by recruiting a number of candidates, some of whom will likely be underqualified and some of whom will likely be overqualified, and placing in the middle of the list the one whom the recruiter feels is the best candidate. This is not a hard-and-fast rule, but it does happen. Many times, the client will hire several candidates on the slate for other positions in the organization. If the client decides on the more overqualified candidate, chances are the fee to the search firm will increase. As a candidate, you will never find out at what point you entered the interview cycle or where you might be positioned on the slate of candidates.

Just because you're working with a search firm doesn't mean you can slow down or stop searching on your own for a job. As a matter of fact, if you continue your search and find a suitable position, you have some bargaining power. If the recruiter doesn't react when told you have another opportunity, you were never a serious candidate for the position.

10. Corporate Recruiters

Understanding Corporate Recruiters

Make three correct guesses consecutively and you will establish a reputation as an expert.

—Laurence J. Peter

Being a corporate recruiter is a little like being an emergency room attending physician. There's always some level of panic when dealing with candidates seeking positions, as well as urgency when handling hiring managers who seek *the one* perfect candidate immediately. Adding to this sense of urgency is the Internet, which vastly expands the resources available for candidates to apply for jobs, overloading recruiters with candidates to review, and the distinct possibility that the hiring company might be conducting a parallel search on its own or with another or multiple other search firms.

The average recruiter receives several hundred resumes and phone contacts a week. Some resumes received are directed to a particular search; others just ask to be placed in the recruiter's database for future searches. Recruiters make quick decisions about who gets seen—often in a matter of seconds. This applies to both corporate recruiters and third-party recruiters like me.

A recruiter has to be able to juggle multiple job assignments at the same time to survive. For example, it is not unusual for a recruiter to be recruiting for ten or even twenty different business disciplines at the same time. For example, in one period last year, I was managing concurrent searches for a marketing vice president, a director of public relations, a CIO, a sales manager, a senior product manager, a software product evangelist, a director of engineering, and a director of worldwide facilities. Each search was a silo project that required a tailored approach and understanding of the position. With one's attention stretched over many recruiting projects, it is imperative that a submitted resume get to the point and grab the attention of the recruiter. The recruiter is simply too busy to mind-read what you might have intended to convey if you didn't state it clearly and succinctly on the resume and cover letter you submitted.

What a Recruiter Thinks About When Meeting a Candidate

Recruiters make snap judgments. We don't have the luxury of time to do otherwise. Give a recruiter an excuse to screen you out and don't be surprised when that's just what happens. So what first impressions do we make when we meet a candidate, either in person or upon viewing a resume?

- If the e-mail address on the resume is badboy@yahoo. com or something similarly suggestive, the individual is not mature or professional.
- If there are misspellings in the resume, the individual can't spell, read, or think about the importance of running a spell-checker before sending us the document.
- If the individual had multiple jobs indicating a tendency to job hop, that behavior will continue.
- If the individual was laid off and it wasn't part of a large-scale layoff, the company cleared out the dead wood.
- People don't change: The past is a great predictor of the future and a candidate's problem will always be a problem.
- This is the best this individual will ever look.

- If the individual was fired in today's business climate, he or she was the problem.
- If looking for a better opportunity, how long is this opportunity going to last?
- If the reason for a job change is money, don't hire.
- The fact that skills are listed on a resume doesn't mean the individual is proficient in any or all of them.
- Time in positions doesn't indicate experience, just time.

11. Making the First Contact

Using Your Phone Power

No one ever listened himself out of a job.

—Calvin Coolidge

Chances are your first contact with a recruiter or potential employer will be by telephone. Opportunities are lost quickly based on the perception created in the first few minutes of the call. The problem with a phone call is that it may be a total surprise when it happens. You are caught off guard and unprepared. Callers, based on your resume, have an image of you in their minds. The interviewer is expecting to hear energy in your voice and enthusiasm in your willingness to talk. Be aware there is a line between enthusiasm and overenthusiasm. Don't cross it. The call is a serious matter; the caller has taken time out of a busy day to contact you because he or she was interested in something seen on your resume. Focus on the conversation. Be serious. Now is not the time to try to make a friend. If the interviewer encounters a slow talker who has to be pressed to respond to questions, the call is quickly terminated.

Formulate Your Answers into Sound Bites

Short and memorable is exponentially better than long and rambling. Practice communicating your answers in short, to-the-point, sound bites. The interviewer can then easily capture your pearls of profundity in their interview notes (which will be sent to the hiring manager). For example, the interviewer will likely ask, "What makes you qualified for this job?" Rather than a rambling response, you might say: "I believe I have three key strengths that make me a good fit for this job: One, I have five years of experience in managing people; two, I have taken projects from conception to completion on time and under budget; and three, I have recruited and developed many excellent staff members who have moved on to higher positions in the organization."

It is imperative that you have several great questions ready to ask the interviewer. Many interviews are decided when the candidate demonstrates an intellectual understanding of the position or challenges the interviewer. Here are a few good questions to consider asking:

A year from now, when you are rating my performance excellence, what will you recall my having accomplished?

Based on our interview, what do you think is lacking in my background to fit this position?

Your voice paints a mental picture of you in the caller's mind. A strong relaxed voice and a sense of humor adds credibility in filling out the caller's mental picture. The caller may not be experienced with conducting phone interviews (hard to believe, but true!) and seeks to fill time until a path is presented or a plan is formulated. The clue to this is being asked to tell him or her about yourself. Before accepting this broad opportunity to ramble, consider leading off with the aspects in your background that apply to the needs of the position. Don't re-read your resume to the caller; that's boring for everyone involved. Remember, you must inspire the caller to invite you for a face-to-face interview.

After covering how your background matches the position, stop speaking and ask if the caller has any questions. This is critical. Candidates have a tendency to get on a roll and dominate the conversation with information they *think* is important and miss the opportunity to gather input from the caller on what is important to the caller. Every time you are asked a question, answer the question concisely, then ask the caller if they would like additional detail. The hard lesson to learn here is to shut up and listen for direction.

Adding Voice Credibility

If you have a home office or a place near the phone to conduct business calls, get a large mirror and put it in back of the phone so you can see yourself when you speak. When you are conducting business or receiving calls, watch your body language, especially your facial movements and expressions. The first time you do this, you will be surprised by what you see. The trick is to always keep a smile on your face; if you do, you will have a smile in your voice. Also, consider dressing up for the call, at least from the waist up. Seeing yourself in the mirror dressed as the professional you are will translate to a behavioral change in your presentation; act as if you are in the face-to-face interview. Dressing in your casual clothes during an important call tells your psyche you are on vacation and during your conversation you may end up sounding too relaxed.

Sound Quality Matters

Speaking of phones, make sure your phone is of high quality with headset capability, and if possible, wireless. Never use a speaker or cellphone when conducting business; it distorts your voice and makes you sound weaker. If you receive a call on your cellphone, ask if you can return the call from a landline in a few minutes to assure you both have the best connection possible. Even if the caller insists on speaking on the cellphone, he or she will respect your effort. I can't even count the number of times I have had telephone conversations with candidates in which poor sound quality and difficulties in communicating factored heavily in the decision not to go forward.

When receiving a call regarding your candidacy, stand up.

You have a higher level of energy and project better standing than sitting. You also have more oxygen reaching your brain because your blood flows better when you're standing. Finally, most people think faster on their feet because they can move their body and arms to better express themselves. Don't forget to have your phone interview in front of the mirror. This is where a wireless headset is priceless.

If you know a call is coming (it's been scheduled by the hiring organization), pull together your points concerning your background and paste them, using individual sticky notes, on your mirror. This way, you'll be reminded of them but you won't sound as though you're reading off your resume. Sounds crazy, I know, but it works.

If you can, make an audio recording of yourself answering questions about your background. Listen to the quality of your answers and your energy as you list and briefly summarize your professional accomplishments. You may be surprised and disappointed with your performance, but now you have a benchmark. Practice and improve your delivery by comparing various recordings of yourself. If you aren't impressed with your delivery, expect the caller to have the same opinion. The time to fix it is before the phone starts ringing. Watch out for the killer "uhs" and "you knows" in your conversation. As you may be aware, it had a negative effect on the appointment of a recent candidate for the U.S. Senate in New York. And just in case it needs saying, I'll say it. Don't use profanity.

When speaking on the phone, don't reach for your cup of coffee or can of fizzy soda. You can drink your beverage before the call or after the call, but not during the call. The same goes for eating.

A good recruiter can look at a person's resume and determine fairly quickly whether the individual has the technical know-how or the right background for a specific job. The tough part is to make an assessment of a candidate over the phone on the deeper issues of personality, cultural fit, and management style. These "gut feel" factors constitute approximately 60 percent of the hiring decision.

I normally script out several questions based on the candidate's resume. Having the questions ready keeps me on track probing the areas of interest. The answers to the questions, voice energy, and the candidate's sense of humor determine the next step—if there is to be one.

A Sample Interview

I typically begin phone interviews by asking if the candidate has any time restrictions on the call. If the candidate has only a short time to speak with me, I reschedule the call to a more suitable time. This may be an indication that the candidate is not serious about the position, so I only do this once per candidate. My time is valuable.

I assume the candidate has reviewed the position specifications prior to the phone interview, and my next question tells me whether my assumption is valid.

> *QUESTION: "Explain this position to me based on your understanding of it, highlighting the important areas that match up with your experience."*

This is a stress question. If the candidate has not reviewed the position or thought about how he or she fits the position, this will be apparent in the candidate's answer (or rambling non-answer). If the candidate has prepared, this is a softball question.

> *QUESTION: "Why are we talking today? What is going on with your current job?"*

I have found this type of question to be helpful in getting to the real reason behind the individual's motivation to change jobs. Being laid off is a common reason to search for a new job, but recruiters know companies rarely lay off their best performers.

> *QUESTION: "As this process develops, one of the things I do is contact your manager to discuss your performance in the position and what effort was made in trying to retain you. If I made that call today, what would your manager tell me?"*

After asking this question, I would listen for any hesitation in the candidate's voice. If I receive pushback, I know there is a problem to be probed.

QUESTION: *"How were you selected for your current/last position? What were the criteria used?"*

What I am listening for is prior performance in a position that earned the candidate the promotion. If the candidate has been in the position for a short period and is looking again, what was the candidate lacking that was missed during that previous selection process?

Recruiters and hiring managers sometimes underestimate the importance of the phone screen in making good hires. In fact, I think it's a key component of the recruiting process. As a guest—that is, not in the role of recruiter—I have sat in on several executive-initiated phone interviews where the call involved three to five managers asking questions of the candidate. The results were as expected; the questions were generic in nature and focused only on the candidate's technical skills. Nobody asked probing questions regarding management style, current performance, or the reason for seeking a new position. At the conclusion of the phone interviews, the panel could not reach a decision on whether to extend an invitation for a face-to-face interview, which was the objective of the phone interview.

If you are a candidate engaged in a phone interview and you get that funny feeling it's not going well, you have to take control or risk missing an excellent opportunity. This can be accomplished by asking questions of the interviewers:

- Take names: At the beginning of the call, when the individuals are introducing themselves, write down their names and titles to get a feel for the level of the interviewers. Use their names occasionally when you respond. It signifies you paid attention to them from the outset of the call.

- Get clarification: Before you answer a question, ask a member of the panel (by name) for clarification. This demonstrates and confirms your level of understanding of the question. This can also be perceived as a stalling technique, so don't do it more than once or twice during the conversation.

- Talk to your strengths: If you are not asked questions that allow you to mention your strong points, weave in the strength whenever possible at the conclusion of your answers.

- Sing your own praise: Work into the conversation a major accomplishment that relates to a question whenever possible.

- Be quick and energetic: Pausing too long before answering the question can give the interviewer the impression you're looking up an answer on Google or can't remember what's on your own resume. A brief pause of a second or two is fine; a pause of ten seconds is not.

12. Presentation Is (Almost) Everything

Dressing for the Interview

Fashion is a form of ugliness so intolerable that we have to alter it every six months.

—*Oscar Wilde*

Not so long ago, any candidate could get an interview and job if he or she just showed up in the lobby somewhere near the appointed time. The demand for talent then was so intense that a candidate's appearance was a secondary consideration at best. Many of those unkempt individuals who found those positions are now back in the market; the economic downturn spurred employers to weed out those misfits who didn't really fit into the company's culture. An interviewer can decide your candidacy in the first ten seconds of meeting you. If you are underdressed for the interview, the decision is reached even more quickly.

Paying attention to how you look in an interview can help you get a job. For that matter, it can also help you keep one. With companies looking everywhere for opportunities to trim overhead, they want to retain those people who best present their firm's image, and that may mean jettisoning the rest. A crisp, businesslike appearance is back in vogue. Prospective employers are looking for a sharper style in their candidates and employees. A proper suit (if that is the accepted uniform in your target industry) that says you are collected and prepared to work is recommended. The old rule of thumb is to always dress at least one level above the position for which you are interviewing. That rule still applies.

The clothes you wear for an interview say a lot about your discipline, taste, and social poise. I recently had a candidate get rejected because he wore brown unshined shoes with a blue suit. In the post-interview meeting, my client kept repeating that one negative: the candidate wore the wrong shoes with the suit. If this had been a back-office position, it might not have mattered, but this was a high-profile position. The concern was that perhaps the candidate was not sensitive enough to the company's image. That particular candidate might have been perfect in every other respect, but his choice of footwear was a deal-breaker and that one lingering doubt in the interviewers' minds prolonged the search process to find another candidate. If you don't know what shoes to wear with a suit (and assuming it's a proper suit, purchased relatively recently at a decent shop), ask the salesperson for some fashion advice.

When preparing for a face-to-face interview, leave nothing to chance. Make sure your hair, nails, and shoes are in tip-top shape. Have your dress or suit professionally pressed. I have always advised candidates to acquire an interviewing uniform (i.e., a new suit or dress—either navy blue or black—that fits well, matched with a new white shirt/blouse and a solid red tie or accent piece—not bright or flashy—and black shoes to complete the look). This is called the "power suit." It commands respect because of its classic, simple appearance. If you don't believe me, watch television and see what the power players wear.

Every hiring company has an unspoken expectation. They expect their new employee to make a key contribution immediately, so the job interview is fundamentally a sales encounter. You are selling a product (yourself) to solve a problem. When the hiring parties meet someone they can easily relate to, someone who is genuine, pleasant, sincere, and appropriately dressed, the interview switches from interviewing to one of selling you on the job.

The first impression you make on a potential employer is the most important one. Before you shake hands or have a chance to answer a question, your interviewer has already made his or her first judgment about you. The first judgment an interviewer makes is based on how you look and what you are wearing. Even if you know the work environment is casual or business casual, your interview appearance should not be.

Make your first impression a great one. If you are absolutely positive that no one in the organization *ever* wears a suit and the official uniform really *is* business casual, then invest in quality business wear—a new button-down shirt with a sport coat or a nice button-down shirt/blouse. Since the casual interviewing clothing may need to be worn several times (and might carry you over into the work setting after you land the job), have them dry-cleaned instead of laundered to keep their new look.

Remember every company has an individual culture. Try to find out what that culture is before the interview, if at all possible. Post-interview meetings with my clients often contain feedback regarding concerns for cultural fit. Again, LinkedIn can be a good place to start your search for information on company culture; send an e-mail message to those LinkedIn members currently or formerly employed by your target company and ask for their feedback on how they perceive the culture. You may be surprised by how much information can be gathered quickly. *Fortune* 100 companies tend to post this sort of detailed information on their Web sites.

When you are scheduled for a face-to-face interview, ask your caller what would be appropriate for the interview. Alternatively, you might want to visit the company in advance of the interview and sit for a few minutes in the lobby; look at how the people entering and exiting are dressed. The marketing materials many companies place in their lobbies may also be helpful in preparing for the interview.

Interview Attire

Men's Interview Attire

- Suit (solid color—navy or dark gray/black)
- Long-sleeved shirt (white, professionally laundered and pressed)
- Belt matching shoes
- Tie (solid red, not bright)
- Dark socks with conservative leather shoes, polished
- Little or no jewelry (watch and ring) (no body piercings or tattoos visible)
- Neat, professional hairstyle; no scruffy beard
- Limit the aftershave
- Neatly trimmed nails
- Portfolio

Women's Interview Attire

- Suit/dress (solid color—navy or dark gray/black)
- Skirt or dress should be long enough so you can sit down comfortably
- Coordinated blouse (white)
- Conservative shoes
- Limited jewelry (no dangling earrings or arms full of bracelets)
- No jewelry is better than cheap jewelry
- Professional hairstyle
- Light makeup and perfume
- Neatly manicured, clean nails
- Portfolio

Interviews can be stressful. It has been said that an employment interview triggers the same level of stress as does a negative employment termination interview. When dressing for an interview, you should be professional but comfortable. When you are comfortable and proud of your appearance, it translates to self-confidence and it shows. Ill-fitting clothes or shoes will add discomfort to a stressful situation; invest in a proper interview suit and shoes that fit you well.

13. The Interview

Interview Preparation

Death will be a great relief. No more interviews.
—Katharine Hepburn

Your executive recruiter should prepare you for your initial face-to-face interview. Some don't and it's a mistake that costs their candidate the job and themselves a commission. If your recruiter doesn't prep you, ask. Recruiters have inside information about positions, the personalities of the interviewers, their expectations, and their vision of what the perfect candidate looks like. Use this knowledge to showcase your abilities. Recruiters who are reluctant to work with you and share this intelligence may not consider you to be their top candidate or may not be fully trusted by their client. In either case, once a company has seen your resume presented by one recruiter, it's too late to change horses. The best you can do is conduct your own research using the various strategies discussed in previous chapters.

Recruiters who present slates of candidates will position you among their other candidates. Recruiters are under no obligation to tell you where you are positioned on the slate, but you can ask. If your recruiter won't tell you, you can always ask the first interviewer how far along the company is in the interview process; he or she might just tell you how many candidates have already been seen and how many more are scheduled.

Those candidates who arrive for the face-to-face interview unprepared, poorly dressed, or with dull interviewing skills have a lower probability of success. Do your homework and press your recruiter to help you.

I've found the best way to help a candidate ace the initial interview is to make sure he or she matches the client's expectations as closely as possible. Expectations include physical appearance and health, speech patterns, sense of humor, alertness, and sense of urgency. If I decide to present the candidate, I discuss with the candidate any areas of concern and make recommendations to improve his or her presentation. For many candidates, particularly senior candidates, it's been a while since they sat on the interviewee's side of the desk.

I give candidates several articles on interviewing if I detect the need for this sort of prep work. I also stress to them the value of reading and practicing the nonverbal language of interviewing (body language) that guides and can salvage a poor interview if properly applied (see section in Chapter 13 on body language).

Interview success requires discovery or, ideally, advance knowledge of what the interviewer is listening for in your answers about experience or skills. This can be accomplished by listening to the question and then verifying your understanding of the question without repeating the question. Then, answer the question concisely and conclude, if possible, with an example from your experience. By using an example of your experience, you subconsciously convince the interviewer that you have the experience.

One piece of interview feedback I hear from clients, and more frequently than I'd like to because it can mean an otherwise potentially great candidate is sunk, is that a candidate showed little or no energy or enthusiasm for the position. When I bring this to the attention of the candidate, the candidate is invariably surprised. Interviewers look for people with "spark," people who will inject new enthusiasm to the position and organization. A way to express this spark is to mention examples of your energy and enthusiasm relating to your current or last position. That leaves the client with the impression that you *have* energy and enthusiasm and might display it once you are in the position for which you're interviewing. Consider this example:

We had a problem with the new product and it looked like we were going to miss the launch date. I didn't wait. I called as many individuals as possible involved in the launch process to an informal meeting, laid out the challenges and opportunities, got their buy-in to help each other as requested/needed, and in two weeks, we were back on schedule to meet the launch date.

No matter how energetic and self-confident you are in the interview, if you are not hands-on and technically sound in your field of expertise, you will not succeed in the interview and, if you do manage to land the job, you won't last in the position. People want to look up and learn from individuals who can teach and elevate them.

Answering Questions

There are two ways to answer interview questions: the short version and the long version. When a question is open-ended, always say, "How much detail would you like?" A pet peeve of recruiters and hiring managers alike is the candidate who says, "Let me give you the short version" and then goes into a lengthy discussion that completely misses the mark. Interviewers will almost always opt for the shorter version, knowing the details are there for probing if needed. Always tailor your answer to what was asked, without rambling on introducing extraneous information. Rambling is an interview killer.

Larry Dillon

Finally, the Face-to-face Meeting

Confidence has a lot to do with interviewing—that, and timing.
—Michael Parkinson

After years of interviewing professionals and executives, I've concluded that interviewing is not an effective process. Interviewing is, in many senses, a likeability contest. The hiring decision factors are too numerous to count, since they vary from company to company and industry to industry. If interviewing were effective, we would not have the same number of failures in management roles. Interestingly, statistical data on hiring failures (assuming it's collected) is rarely published. Many HR studies over the years have determined that people fail in positions because of personal chemistry or work culture; lack of skill is hardly, if ever, mentioned. Based on this information, one would assume interviewing questions would be focused on these two important elements.

When I ask hiring managers about their critical wants and needs regarding the position they seek to fill, 90 percent of the time their list includes personal chemistry and work culture. But, when debriefing candidates after their interviews with the organization, I discover the interviewers have asked no questions related to either topic. Instead, interviewers ask skill-related questions, because skill questions are simple to understand: You either have the skill or you don't. Technical skills, work history, and academic degrees are easy to verify, but how do you determine a person's personal chemistry and work culture—the person's ability to fit in with the rest of the company? The answer is a series of interviews to assess "likeability." In a way, it's like applying to an exclusive club; what determines acceptance could be the cut of a person's suit.

This suggestion will never be accepted, but I offer it because it's logical and, in practice, it works. Only the recruiter meets with the candidate, rather than inviting a candidate in to interview with a hiring team for the position. If the candidate passes the recruiter, the candidate is then asked for his or her references in advance.

I always ask for fifteen references made up of managers, supervisors, employees, and peers, as well as customers, if the position is an outward-focused one. Then I conduct an extensive interview of the references to determine the candidate's personal chemistry and work culture, as well as the candidate's skills, in that order. In my book, *Finding Heroes*, I laid out how to do this verification process. It wouldn't kill you to think about what your managers, supervisors, employees, and peers would say about you.

Each time I have applied this unusual methodology and presented the results to the hiring team, the interviewing process was seamless and quick because the only unknown factor was the candidate's technical skills, which are easy to determine.

Back to Reality—the Interviewing Process

The interviewing process varies depending on the company or organization; some employers prefer a formal process, while others tend to view it as a personality contest. Normally, when invited in to interview, the scheduling individual will forward to you the location, time, and a list of the individuals you will be meeting. If the schedule includes the list of interviewers, this is a plus for you. You have the opportunity to research the individuals to get an understanding of their backgrounds and possible connections to people you may know. Interviewers are impressed when the candidate has researched them prior to meeting them. I do caution candidates to be careful how they inject this information into the conversation. The best way is to reference their experience to support your answer to their question. For example:

> *"Yes, I did take the lead in the project. It was a new technology for us and failure would be costly. I saw this opportunity as a challenge, not a risk, based on my previous project management experience, similar to what you took on at Ellco Corporation."*

The First Interviewer

Let's start at the beginning of your interviewing day. You arrive fifteen minutes early in the lobby, not earlier. Fifteen minutes allows enough time to sign in and decompress a little. You don't want to arrive sooner than fifteen minutes early because, when the receptionist announces your presence to the first interviewer, it puts a little pressure on him or her to hurry up and finish whatever else they're doing and to meet with you. Interviewers want to impress you with their organization and do not want to make you wait. Arriving earlier than expected may not be a problem, but starting off on the wrong foot by having irritated your interviewer with a really early arrival is unnecessary and avoidable.

While you wait in the lobby, take the opportunity to observe the company dynamics. The lobby is, after all, a microcosm of the corporate culture. If people are friendly and open, chances are this is an open culture where personalities are appreciated. On the other hand, if the lobby is quiet and people enter and exit with little dialogue or laughter, this is a formal, structured company. Knowing the company dynamics can help you tailor your presentation during the interview. You can confirm this impression on meeting with the first interviewer. If the interviewer personally meets you in the lobby and escorts you to an office or conference room, this could be a signal this organization is people friendly; continue to observe the surroundings to confirm your approach to the interview. If, on the other hand, you are escorted to the interviewer's office or a conference room by a member of the administrative staff, chances are you are in a formal setting; behave accordingly.

Small Talk and Controlling the Interview

The first few minutes of the interview process can be the entire interview. The introduction can sometimes be a little awkward. After the customary handshake, offer your current business card; if you are unemployed, have some cards made up with your contact information and, more importantly, ask for the interviewer's card. Don't be surprised if he or she doesn't have a card handy if you're not meeting in his or her office. Many interviewers prefer not to give out their card with their direct contact information, but you certainly won't get a card if you don't ask for one. Having the interviewer's card makes it easier to send a thank you note.

Understand both parties want to impress the other person and control the meeting. The interviewer is asking himself or herself whether you are the person who was expected, appearance-wise, and whether you will fit in the organization.

If the interview is held in the interviewer's office, quickly check the surroundings to confirm the status of the individual. Family pictures and sporting memorabilia may be on display, adding to your information about the interviewer. The more senior the individual, the nicer his or her office furnishings. If you want to comment on anything in the interviewer's office, wait until the end of the interview. Don't waste your interviewing time; the interview has a set time limit and wasted time discussing unrelated topics diminishes the value of the interview and the interviewer's perception of you.

Most interviewers will offer a beverage upon meeting with you. Because time for interviewing is limited, always decline. Time spent fetching a beverage is time not available for questions and answers, and half-empty cups of cold coffee get in the way on the desk.

While in the interview, your posture is important. When seated, sit up straight and do not cross your legs. Leaning back in the chair and crossing your legs sends a signal of complacency, not one of a high-energy professional. When answering a question, always lean slightly forward with both feet on the ground and looking directly at the interviewer. You may not be aware that many interviewees, when formulating an answer to a question, look away from the interviewer. This is the way many individuals solve problems, by daydreaming a bit, but it conveys to the interviewer that you are concealing information or making up an answer because you are not looking directly at the interviewer. I don't mean you should stare unblinkingly into the interviewer's eyes. Some cultures interpret this gesture as an insult.

One thing that always triggers a red flag in my mind and presumably in the minds of interviewers is the candidate who sits down and immediately pulls out his or her resume or a writing pad on which to take notes. What this says to me is that the candidate is not sure of all the information on the resume because it's been embellished or that he or she needs time to formulate answers to questions. In either case, this behavior signals a candidate who is not prepared to discuss his or her background because it may not be truthful. Never take notes or have anything in your hands or lap. Interviewers recognize this behavior as a stall technique and it's an interview killer.

I once conducted an interview where the candidate immediately sat down, crossed his legs, pulled out both the resume and a large notebook, and started reading his resume to me. I sat there for a few minutes without saying a word. Eventually, the candidate stopped reading and showed me a puzzled look. He asked me if I had any questions and I replied no. I asked him what questions he had of me, since he was conducting the interview. I asked him to put away his materials, which he did. I then told him I had only one question that needed answering: Based on his understanding of the position, what were the three critical skill needs in the position and would he compare those skill needs against his experience. The candidate sat there for a few minutes, then got up and walked out. He either did not understand the needs of the position or he knew he did not have the background. At least he didn't waste too much of my time.

The interviewer's first question is important. Normally, it is a general question to open the conversation. Many interviewers have a set of standard questions they use in any interview situation; this is a fallback strategy for individuals who do not interview often or do not know how to interview. Interestingly enough, most management people interview less than 5 percent of their time and are not good at it. This is a disadvantage to the candidate, because an interviewer who does not know what to ask will likely make a decision based on gut feelings and personality.

If you get the feeling the interviewer isn't touching on the important aspects of your background, you must discreetly and covertly assume control of the interview and steer the conversation in your favor. It's not as difficult as it sounds. At the end of an answer and before the interviewer can ask the next question, state the following: "I've been giving this opportunity a great deal of thought and would like, if I may, to contrast my experience and background against what I feel are the real needs of the position. I'd appreciate your input on my assessment." Unless the interviewer is a stickler for adhering to his or her set pattern of questions, this should be acceptable, since you ended your statement by asking the interviewer to critique your comments.

Given permission to demonstrate your knowledge of the position, you need to concisely and cleverly weave in your relevant skills, experience, and results of your actions that match the needs of the position. The interviewer is listening for how you solved the problem and trying to figure out whether that approach would work in the position for which you're interviewing. To be able to demonstrate your abilities, you need to have carefully thought through this possible scenario and rehearsed the response, so it comes across unrehearsed and concise. If your presentation isn't concise and to the point, the interviewer will interrupt you and reestablish control of the interview. If you do the work for him or her by precisely matching the position's needs with your own experience, you will likely maintain control of the interview.

The purpose of any question is to find a reason to confirm the interviewer's initial gut feeling, whether it's positive or negative, about your candidacy. When answering a multi-part question, listen to the questions and answer them to the best of your abilities in the order in which the various parts were asked. I observed some time ago that very intelligent candidates always answered my questions in the order asked; the less brilliant candidates answered them in reverse order. Both ways are acceptable, but it is an indication of how each candidate processes data. The candidates who answer questions in the same order as they were asked tend to get the job offers more often than those who answer questions in reverse order.

When confronted with a question you cannot answer, the best answer is to state you do not have the answer. Don't try to dream up an answer on the spot. Interviewers respect honesty and have been known to ask stretch questions to gauge your reaction.

Don't over answer a question. It's a surefire way to kill an interview. Don't talk yourself out of contention for the position.

When responding to a question, respond concisely and end with, "I can expand with further details if you're interested." This keeps the interview moving along at a nice, consistent pace. Understandably, you are excited about your experience and background and want the interviewer to know as much about you as possible in the time allotted for the interview, but trust the interviewer to have plenty of questions to fill the time and probe for the information he or she wants to gather from you.

When answering a challenging question, it's acceptable to say to the interviewer, "That's an excellent question," and then make sure you understand the question before responding, but don't use this ploy more than twice in an interview. If you do, the interviewer will feel you are patronizing him or her while stalling for time to fabricate an answer.

If I Was Conducting the Interview

Consider this example of how I, as an executive recruiter, conduct an interview. I always meet candidates in the lobby and escort them to my office. This gives me a few minutes to size up the candidate before sitting down to conduct an interview. I do not offer a beverage because I want to keep the focus on the interview. I will spend three to five minutes in small talk, which helps the candidate get settled.

I normally do a three-phase interview consisting of qualifying, skill set, and management style questions. An issue in any phase ends the interview. For this demonstration, I will only use a few questions.

The First Question

"Tell me how you prepared for this interview. What type of research did you do?"

I would then just sit back and listen to the answer. What I expect to hear is an in-depth answer citing the facts related to the company and the position and possibly some areas of concern or questions that need to be answered about the position. If questions are posed to me, I put them off until the wrap-up portion of the interview. I never cede control of the interview to the candidate, which is what happens if the discussion is allowed to shift to answering the candidate's questions.

The Second Question

"Since our time together is short, what are the three things in your background and experience that directly apply to this position?"

What I am expecting to hear is a review of similar experiences, dovetailing them with the facts and issues of this position and possible lessons learned. This is the opportunity for the candidate to impress the interviewer with like experiences and, with luck, touch on all the critical skill needs of the position.

The Third Question

"Why were you selected for your current/last position? What were the criteria?"

The focus of this question is your job performance, what it was, and what you did that was exceptional to get selected.

The Fourth Question

"Which business-related accomplishment are you the most proud of?"

This question is meant to elicit your take on which business accomplishments were important and why. Just because it was important to you doesn't mean it was important to the employer and, whether or not you realize it, your answer will telegraph the difference.

Follow-up Questions

What role did you play?
Who was involved?
What was the financial impact on the organization?
What were the downside risks?
How were you recognized for this accomplishment?

Body Language

Nonverbal Communication

No single motion ever stands alone.

—*Ray L. Birdwhistell*

There are two parts to an interview. Most candidates prepare for an interview by rehearsing their answers to possible questions, but fail to prepare for the nonverbal aspects of the interview. In an interview situation, Dr. Birdwhistell found that 65 percent of social meaning is conveyed by body language; more than half the message received and sent will be visual rather than verbal.

The importance of visual information in any exchange and why success depends more on silent speech than auditory systems is evidenced by the fact that, when faced with the hypothetical alternative of going either deaf or blind, more than 95 percent of people opt for deafness. Hearing is highly efficient at up to twenty feet, while one-way communication is possible from up to one hundred feet away, so long as the speaker speaks slowly. The eye can detect tremendously detailed information from one hundred feet away, and remains effective for human communications at a distance of a mile. As a result, the information provided by our eyes tends to be far more precise and much less ambiguous than that available through our ears. This suggests that, as information gatherers, our eyes are one thousand times more effective than our ears.

The more you know about the silent language, the more effective you can be in any interpersonal relationship. Learning to listen to the spoken word while watching to see if the visual language matches what is being said is a learned skill. In interviews, candidates and hiring managers visually telegraph their questions and answers before uttering them. We constantly send visual messages, sometimes only 1/25 of a millisecond in length. When stressed, we might tug at our ears, wring our hands, or touch our faces. These unconscious gestures can be construed as a method of buying time to think about a question. In days gone by, a candidate might light up a cigarette or sip from a cup of coffee as a means of buying time to think about a response.

The subject of the candidate's body language is rarely discussed. Trained interviewers watch the candidate's eyes and limbs throughout the interview for indications of how the candidate reacts to questions; reactions can be more telling than the candidate's answers. For example, candidates who look to the ceiling when first responding to a question have visual natures and work best when a picture can be formed in their mind. Hands to the face around the mouth or looking away from the interviewer may be indicators of some doubt in the answer.

Observe interviewers closely when they ask a question; look at their face first to see if the expression goes with what is being said. Then, listen to the tone of voice for possible hidden meanings. Finally, listen to the spoken words. Interviewers at times can become so focused in developing the next question that they don't listen to the answer. If the interviewer does not maintain eye contact with you during your answer, you may be losing the interview because you lost the interviewer's attention. There's a simple trick to get the interviewer's attention: just touch your nose. The simple movement of your hand to the nose forces the interviewer to look at you.

The Secret Language

Many books and articles have been written on the subject of body language. They are well worth reviewing as part of your preparation for an interview. In the meantime, I offer these highlights of the art of interpreting nonverbal messages and managing behavior that can control an interview.

79

Watch the Interviewer's Eyes

We all think we watch people's eyes but, in reality, we don't. The appropriate technique in interviewing is to watch the eyes of the interviewer as the question is being asked. If your answer isn't what was expected, puzzlement will be displayed in an interviewer's eyes for a split second at the conclusion of your answer; this split-second reaction gives some indication of the interviewer's understanding of your answer, which may call for a restatement of your answer.

No matter what a person says, his or her eyes will tell you what he or she is really thinking. If the interviewer's pupils widen, then something pleasant was said; you've made the interviewer feel good by your comments. If the pupils contract, then something you have said struck a nerve. If the interviewer's eyes narrow into a squint, then they're not buying what you're selling.

Watch Where the Interviewer Looks

You can assess whether an interviewer is an extrovert or introvert based on where the interviewer looks when listening to a response. If the interviewer looks up and to the left, then the interviewer is extroverted and sees big pictures (as opposed to big details). Looking down and to the right indicates a more introverted individual who thinks in details and numbers. This is good information to have because, armed with this knowledge, you can tailor your answers. Extroverts like things painted in images because of their visual nature. Introverts like facts and numbers in the answers; they are more comfortable with hard data than with fuzzy concepts.

Nod Your Head

Nodding of the head is the most common nonverbal method of communication. We do it without thinking. A rapid head nod indicates, "hurry up and finish." A slow nod indicates, "I understand, keep going, I'm interested in what you're saying." Learn to sometimes pace your answers in response to the interviewer's head nods. A slow nod from the interviewer signals, "tell me more." A fast nod indicates, "enough, let's move on."

Test with Your Eyebrows

Try watching an interview on television with the volume turned down. The impact of the movement of the eyebrows is dynamic between the interviewer and interviewee. We cannot easily control the reaction movement of our eyebrows, and each movement communicates a message. Raising one eyebrow in response to a statement means the listener doesn't believe what's just been said. Lifting both eyebrows indicates surprise. The interviewer who raises his or her eyebrows while asking a question is telegraphing that there is an expected answer and only one such answer to the question.

Interviewers Watch the Mouth

Wetting of the lips throughout the interview may indicate stalling or a high stress level; white spittle in the corners of the mouth is another big indicator of stress. Touching of the mouth when answering a question may also indicate untruthfulness in the answer. An additional sign of increasing stress is the formation of sweat on the upper lip, especially if the interview is conducted in a climate-controlled environment.

Touching of the Nose, Ears, and Eyes

We all touch our faces unconsciously, but it is uncommon to do so in an interviewing situation. Pulling at an ear might indicate a high level of stress in the interview. Interviewers watch if the candidate rubs his or her nose while saying he or she understands; if so it probably means he or she doesn't understand what is being asked. Touching of the eyes may indicate a desire to deceive. If the interviewer touches his or her face after you've answered a question, it's an indicator of concern or doubt about your answer.

Reading the Forehead

Like the eyebrows, movement of the forehead sends a message. If the interviewer wrinkles his or her forehead downward in a frown, it means a problem with what is being said or puzzlement. If the forehead is wrinkled upward, it indicates surprise at what the interviewer has just said or asked.

Watch the Shoulders

A shoulder slump, assuming the interviewer has no physical problems, may indicate indifference to the interview or the interviewer's communications. This behavior is more readily noticed when the interviewer is standing rather than seated.

Watch the Fingers

Finger drumming indicates nervousness or impatience with the process. Seeing this behavior in an interviewer is a clear signal that you are losing the interview. In order to control their fingers, some candidates will hold a copy of the resume; they may or may not refer to the resume. Rather than holding your resume, particularly if your hands are sweaty, try just folding your hands together on your lap.

Watch the Arms

Arms folded across the chest indicate the listener is not buying what the speaker is selling. Normally, this behavior is exhibited when standing. If the interviewer folds his or her arms, this is a powerful signal that things are not going well. The interview is essentially over when this behavior is exhibited.

Listen to Rate of Speech

Speaking quickly may indicate excitement. Slower speech may indicate disinterest in the subject at hand. This is the time to adopt the interviewer's cadence to better fit the interviewing pattern.

Mirror Movements

This behavior sometimes happens without the interviewer being aware of it. Slowly mirroring the body movements of the interviewer has a tendency to relax the interviewer and aid in development of a positive feeling and rapport. The trick is not to move in sync with the interviewer; allow a few seconds to pass before you mimic each movement. Also, watch closely to see whether you're being mirrored. It can lull you into a false sense of security that the interview is going well and make you forget to be professional, concise, and enthusiastic.

Watch the Legs

Legs are difficult to observe in most interviewing situations, especially if the setting involves a table or desk. Interviewers watch to see if you sit forward in your chair or sit back and cross your legs. Sitting back with the legs crossed sends the wrong message to the interviewer. It says, "Impress me." Sitting forward indicates an eagerness to engage in the conversation.

Make a Good Impression and Make It Fast

How long does it take to make a good impression? Some think it takes time, but the evidence suggests that the upper limit is around four or five minutes. Still, many would argue it requires an encounter of less than 120 seconds, because we rapidly give away volumes of information with our faces. The facial action coding system, the result of Paul Ekman's doctoral research, suggests there are forty-three facial movements capable of producing three thousand possible combinations of human emotion. If we can recognize and interpret these various expressions, we can determine whether a person is lying.

Neil Anderson, PhD, at the University of Amsterdam, conducted a study asking participant interviewers to watch videotaped simulated interviews. After four minutes, the tape was stopped and the participants assessed the candidates' personalities and documented their impressions. Then, the videotape was played to its conclusion and another assessment of the candidates' impressions was made. None of the participant interviewers changed their opinions based on their first impressions, made after only 4 minutes.

First impressions are crucial in interviewing. When you think about it, in the first few minutes of the interview, it is the interviewer who does most of the talking and sets the ground rules for the interview. Consequently, the interviewee is nonverbally active, responding through cues such as eye contact, facial expressions, head nods, and gestures. Once we have made a judgment about whether we like the other person, this conclusion is resistant to change. Rather than alter our opinion, we distort subsequent information in a way that makes it support our initial assumptions.

Albert Mehrabian, PhD, professor emeritus (psychology) at the University of California Los Angeles, calculated that only 7 percent of understanding is derived from what is actually said. Thirty-eight percent comes from the tone of voice in which it is said, and 55 percent comes from silent speech signals.

The late Ray L. Birdwhistell, PhD, professor of communications at the University of Pennsylvania, Annenberg School of Communication, estimated that the average individual actually uses words for only ten to eleven minutes daily, with the standard spoken sentence lasting around two and a half seconds. He considered that, when two people are conversing, less than 30 percent of their communication is verbal; more than 65 percent of the social meaning is conveyed by silent signals.

This is why understanding nonverbal communication is critical in your interviewing success; sometimes, before you have uttered a word, the decision has been made in the interviewer's mind. If it's the wrong decision—that is, one not in your favor—then you will need every nonverbal communications skill you have to reverse the decision.

14. Interview Dining

You can tell a lot about a fellow's character by the way he eats jelly beans.

—Ronald Reagan

Interviewing can be even more stressful when you are expected to eat and talk at the same time. One of the reasons employers take job candidates out to lunch or dinner is to evaluate their social skills and to see if they can handle themselves gracefully under pressure.

Interviewers watch what the candidate orders to gauge the candidate's political smarts in preparing for the interview. I once had a candidate order a full slab of ribs for lunch along with two side dishes. It was impossible to carry on a conversation because the candidate never paused in his eating. When he finished, he pushed back the dishes and asked what I would like to know about him. I told him I had all the information I needed and got up and left. I always arrange in advance to have the bill put on my credit card, including the tip. This arrangement allows a parting without any delays or awkward moments.

When you are invited to lunch, never order any alcoholic beverages, even if the interviewer does. This is a test for some interviewers. If you are invited to meet for drinks after normal business hours, be very careful because this is an out of the ordinary interviewing process. This may be a way to see if, after you've had a few drinks, you might reveal what's behind the mask.

When the server asks for your order, try to stall to allow the host to order first. Normally, the host will order light in order to carry on a conversation. Follow his or her lead and do the same. An old trick some recruiters use when interviewing candidates over a meal is to wait until the candidate picks up his or her fork or spoon and then ask them a question. In responding to the questions, the candidate's meal goes to waste and creates additional stress on the candidate, which is what is intended. If you sense this is happening, suggest to the interviewer that he or she defer asking questions until you both finish the meal, so you both can have a more focused discussion. This approach succeeds in most situations and, in a sense, you have taken over the interview, which is a positive.

During the Meal:
- Never order messy food—pasta with lots of sauce, chicken with bones, ribs, or big sandwiches.
- Never order the most expensive entree on the menu.
- Order food that is easy to cut into bite-sized pieces.
- If you need to leave the table, put your napkin on the seat or the arm of your chair.
- When you've finished, move your knife and fork to the "four o'clock" position so the server knows you're done.
- Let the prospective interviewer pick up the tab. You may feel you should offer to split the check, but offering actually diminishes your status. If a recruiter/hiring manager mentions splitting the check, reassess the quality of the opportunity. You were invited, and the person who invited you should pick up the check.

Because the purpose of the meeting is both social testing and assessment of your qualifications, it becomes a balancing act. You will need to use your best interview skills in responding to questions, while displaying your table manners. I once had a candidate taken out for dinner with a CEO as the closing step prior to making an offer. They completed their dinner and walked outside the restaurant, when the candidate noticed the CEO still had his napkin tucked in his waistband. The candidate pointed out the napkin to the CEO, who was embarrassed about having made such a terrible faux pas; he threw the napkin on the ground and walked away. The next morning, the CEO called me to say he did not feel the candidate was a good fit for the position and wanted to see more candidates. My assessment was he knew that if he hired the candidate, and the candidate mentioned the napkin incident to others, the CEO would lose face. If, on the other hand, the candidate hadn't mentioned the napkin and they had parted without the CEO discovering the napkin until later, the same outcome would have resulted. Had the roles been reversed and the candidate had been the one with his napkin in his waistband, the results would have been the same: no job. The point being that there will be times, despite your best efforts, when luck is not on your side.

15. The Offer

Evaluating an Offer

A job offer is not the end of the job search; it's just the beginning of the next job search. Just like an interview, the job offer, when it comes, will tell you a great deal about your potential employer. An offer can reveal how important the employer feels you are to the organization and, if poorly constructed, indicates a lack of respect for your abilities. Some offers may leave you with the feeling that you are not what they were looking for and if you do not accept, they will move on to another candidate. The first indication that you are not their first choice might be a lower title for the position or a reduced salary and bonus than was discussed or advertised.

Jobs are customarily offered verbally over the telephone or sometimes in person, with the written offer sent by mail. The employer should offer more than just, "Congratulations, you've got the job." The presenter should explain and sell the offer in detail and answer your questions. If the offer is below your expectations when it is being presented, you need to challenge the reasoning behind the offer. There will be times when budget constraints or salary caps require the hiring manager to offer a lower salary than expected. If the compensation is close to your original expectation and the title remains the same, chances are it's a serious offer.

The names and titles of your immediate supervisors also should be mentioned in the offer letter. By this time you should have met your manager and perhaps his or her manager during your interview and have gotten acquainted with them. You'll be working with your manager every day, so it's important to feel comfortable around him or her.

Titles Are Important

Don't let anybody convince you your title isn't important. It is. It tells others within and beyond the organization where you are in the pecking order. It also sets you up for your next position, whether that's in this organization or another one. Titles are more than words; they are a short, strategic, and functional explanation of your job and its responsibilities. You need to be clear on your duties so that you know what is expected of you, which can help minimize surprises after you start working. If the title in the offer letter has been lowered from the original position, this should be a red flag to you. Even if the compensation has not changed, this is a valid reason to decline the offer.

Great titles are hard to come by. Think about it. There's only one president, one CEO, and one CFO in most organizations. There may be multiple executive vice presidents and managers, but aim high. If you fail to get the title you expected at the high point of your bargaining power, it could take years to obtain it. Career advancements in titles and compensation are only gained when the employer needs your help solving their problems. Once you are on board, you have lost any bargaining power you might have had. Understand employers have spent months, in most cases, searching for you, and a great deal of money in expenses and management time to get to this offer point. They would rather make a small capitulation instead of starting over for the sake of a title or some additional compensation.

It takes courage to press an employer for additional compensation when you are in need of a position, but if properly handled, you can succeed while winning the hiring manager's respect. A hiring manager normally does not want to be involved in the job offering process. They believe any negative feelings generated will affect the working relationship, and they're

89

probably right. The task is normally delegated to the HR people.

Your response to a mediocre offer has to communicate great respect for the company, its management, and the opportunity, but clearly indicate that what you can offer and accomplish for them is worth more consideration than was presented in the offer. While you are negotiating with the HR people, make sure you stay in touch with the hiring manager via e-mail. You need to reaffirm your interest in the position and mention some possible solutions you can bring to the organization. Having represented many clients in the offering process, I can assure you that this strategy works. More times than I can remember, even against my recommendation, the client added additional compensation in the form of base salary, signing bonus, stock options, or some type of a hiring bonus to come close to what the candidate requested. Rarely did the client actually meet the candidate's target compensation, but always came close, so as to not appear weak but still not have to start the search process all over again.

Compensation

The compensation package is the most important piece of the job offer. This is normally covered in the vetting process by the recruiter when he or she asks about your compensation expectations. If your requirements are not in line with the compensation being offered for the position, you would not be in consideration for the position and wouldn't have been interviewed.

One question that you need to ask involves the timing of your future salary review—in other words, when will you be eligible for a raise and what type of performance review does the organization conduct for individuals at your level. Your salary review normally is tied to your performance review and is a chance for the employer to recognize and reward you for your accomplishments. Generally, the review will take place one year from your start date.

Bonuses

Nowadays, bonuses are standard fare for most organizations. Sometimes they're only offered to key managers or those at the highest level of the organization. When your offer includes mention of a bonus, be sure to clarify the structure, criteria, and limits of the bonus system for your proposed bonus. Employers should tell you about the different bonuses offered, which can be based on personal performance or tied to the company's profits. Sometimes a bonus simply will be a set percentage of your base pay. If you were offered a signing bonus, be sure to ask about the details, such as the date you will receive the payment. Signing bonuses have become commonplace at many progressive companies. Never be afraid to ask for a little more when receiving a signing bonus. I completed seventy-three placements for a high technology company, the majority of which included a signing bonus. Every candidate who received an offer and asked if the hiring bonus could be increased, got it increased. It never hurts to ask, but always do it in a positive way.

The Benefits Package

Compensation isn't just the cash; it's also the benefits. The most important benefits are health and dental insurance, and in some cases, life insurance and 401K. You should find out the name of the provider and the types of coverage you will receive and add this information to your overall evaluation of the offer. You should also be aware how much your insurance will cost each week, and how much your employer will cover. Companies offer different kinds of coverage, and if your company makes you pay more, you have an incentive to negotiate for a higher salary or a bigger bonus to compensate.

Medical plans sometimes take more than a week to process, so find out whether your new medical plan will take effect on the day you start working. Your health insurance plan at your current job may expire on the day you leave or through the paid-up period, but many employers today are making medical insurance effective on your start date. If not, check with your current insurance carrier about an extension of benefits. If your

91

new plan will not take effect right away and you elect to purchase your old plan, you may want to ask your new employer to pay part or all of the plan's premiums until the new one takes effect.

Remember, you want an offer that matches your current employment status, but don't get hung up on comparing health plans as a criterion for accepting a job. Health plans are fixed in concrete for set periods of time. Asking for benefits that are not available for all employees will generate a pushback from the employer and a possible retraction of the offer. When I run into a candidate who is more focused on the benefits than the opportunity, I reject the candidate.

Stock Options

Some companies, both public and private, offer stock options as part of the compensation package. If you are offered options, you will be told verbally and it will be in the written offer. The details of vesting, which are normally provided in the offer letter, identify when an employee has the right to exercise options (purchase and sell shares of stock). Vesting schedules vary from company to company. Be sure to ask when the vesting period begins. You may, for example, become vested in 25 percent of your stock options after each year of employment. It's also in your best interest to know your exercise price, the current price of public stock, and the number of shares outstanding to calculate the value of your options and get a better idea of your total package.

Perqs

Traditionally, some companies offer added perqs (short for perquisites) to executives and some senior managers. If you are eligible for these benefits, they will be disclosed as part of your offer and are not negotiable. They could include memberships to country clubs, air travel upgrades, or a car, just to name a few. Not all companies offer these services, and not all employees are granted these perqs. If you aren't offered them, don't ask for them.

Vacations

Don't forget to ask about the all-important vacation time. Always ask when you are in doubt—never assume—because policies differ from company to company. Generally, every employee receives two weeks of vacation time each year; the number is usually higher for senior-level positions. Vacation time also is sometimes negotiable especially if you are offered less time compared with what you have at your current job. But, many companies have firm policies concerning vacations and expect new hires to conform to their policy. The fact you were able to grow your vacation time to four or eight weeks with your current employer is not your new employer's problem. If you need the same vacation time, you should only interview with companies that offer this benefit. Many companies will consider giving you more time off if the extra time is non-paid.

All offers have a time limit for acceptance; failing to respond on time will automatically cancel the offer, in most cases. Employers are excited when making an offer. They are expecting an enthusiastic response and when the response is less than *"wow!"*, it diminishes the positive impact for the employer, triggering some doubts about the candidate. It is important to be gracious and enthusiastic when you receive an offer. Say positive things about the company and the management group you may be joining. Employers expect you to review the offer and respond within the designated time period and contact them if you have questions.

One thing I would advise is not to state that you will review the offer with your spouse and get back to them. This is a given, but it conveys a weakness on your part to reach a decision, which brings in to question your ability to make decisions without consulting others on the job.

Next Steps

The best advice on how to overcome a job loss and turn it into a success doesn't always work for everyone for the simple reason that we all view the world through different prisms. In a competitive world, an individual's experience, culture, education, and motivation all contribute to a successful job search or, in some cases, disappointment. It can be difficult to continue the pursuit for a new position with the same zeal you had the first day of your search after months of rejection. It's disappointing to not get a callback or any response to your well-crafted resume, but life's winners are those who refuse to give up and wake up every day with at least one new idea to try as part of the job search strategy.

Over the years, I have noticed a recurring pattern with individuals searching for new positions. There always seem to be long periods of rejection and then two or three things start to fall into place at the same time. Seemingly overnight, you are being wooed by several corporate suitors vying for your services. Don't panic. There is no need to decide anything in a hurry. Evaluate all of your options carefully in terms of your needs and future aspirations. The challenge of searching for a job over a long period of time can reshape what you thought was important.

The current situation is unpredictable. Every generation faces uncertain times. Some are worse than others. Still, we have to believe, since we have been here before many times, that we will survive and recover. One small benefit is that since everyone has felt the impact of the worldwide downturn, there is a better appreciation for those out of work. Employers are more understanding and willing to take a chance on someone, whereas just a short while back, that would not have happened.

Appendices: Preparation Resources

Sometimes questions are more important than answers.
—Nancy Willard

It's virtually impossible to guess what types of interview questions might be asked in an interview unless you have interviewed with the same individuals before. Interviewers tend to adopt a questioning methodology that fits their personality and mirrors the corporate culture; they have a set of questions that they use in most of their interviews. For example: Microsoft asks questions to see how you think through a problem. How would you answer these questions?

- Why is a manhole cover round?

- How many cars are there in the United States? (A popular variation on this question is, "How many gas stations are there in the United States?")

- How many manhole covers are there in the United States?

- You've got someone working for you for seven days and a gold bar with which to pay them. The gold bar is segmented into seven connected pieces. You must pay the person working for you at the end of every day. If you are allowed to make only two breaks in the gold bar, how do you pay the worker?

- One train leaves Los Angeles at 15 mph heading for New York. Another train leaves New York at 20 mph heading for Los Angeles on the same track. If a bird, flying at 25 mph, leaves Los Angeles at the same time as the train and flies back and forth between the two trains until they collide, how far will the bird have traveled?

- Imagine a disk spinning like a record player turntable. Half of the disk is black and the other is white. Assume you have an unlimited number of color sensors. How many sensors would you have to place around the disk to determine the direction the disk is spinning? Where would they be placed?

- Imagine an analog clock, the hands of which are positioned to indicate twelve o'clock. Note that the hour and minute hands overlap. How many times each day do both the hour and minute hands overlap? How would you determine the exact times of the day that this occurs?

- You have two jars, fifty red marbles, and fifty blue marbles. A jar will be picked at random, and *then* a marble will be picked from the jar. Placing all of the marbles in the jars, how can you maximize the chances of a red marble being picked? What are the exact odds of getting a red marble using your scheme?

- Pairs of prime numbers separated by a single number are called prime pairs. For example, 17 and 19 are prime numbers, separated by 18. Prove that the number between a prime pair is always divisible by 6 (assuming both numbers in the pair are greater than 6). Now prove that there are no "prime triples."

- There is a room with a door (closed) and three lightbulbs. Outside the room, there are three switches connected to the bulbs. You may manipulate the switches as you wish, but once you open the door, you can't change them. Identify each switch with its bulb.

- Suppose you had eight billiard balls, and one of them was slightly heavier than the others, but the only way to tell was by putting it on a balance scale with another ball on the opposite pan. What's the fewest number of times you'd have to use the scale to find the heavier ball?

- Imagine you are standing in front of a mirror, facing it. Raise your left hand. Raise your right hand. Look at your reflection. When you raise your left hand, your reflection raises what appears to be its right hand. But when you tilt your head up, your reflection does too; it does not appear to tilt its head down. Why is it that the mirror appears to reverse left and right, but not up and down?

- You have four jars of pills. Each pill is the same weight, except for contaminated pills contained in one jar; each contaminated pill is the standard weight + 1. How could you tell which jar had the contaminated pills in just one measurement?

The reason for listing some of Microsoft's questions is not to give you an inside edge on your interview there (you will notice I have not provided the answers), but to point out the sophistication of questions being used in today's recruiting organizations. These types of questions are interspersed with traditional, less tricky questions in some interviews.

There are many approaches to developing interview questions. This section offers examples of various categories of questions common to interviewing situations. Interviewers, depending on the position for which you are presenting yourself, may ask questions from multiple categories depending on the critical aspects of the position. The objective of this tactic is to cover your skills, management style, and potential fit into the organization.

The questions are organized according to the various areas an interviewer might decide to probe. One popular approach is a focus on position attributes, of which there are twenty-nine. Examples of position attributes include decision making, goal setting, and planning. Although you might not think of them this way, these are the hard skills that are easy to probe; either you have the skill or you don't. An interviewer will know your level of expertise in a matter of a few questions. Because the answers to these questions can dismiss you from consideration quickly, interviewers tend to focus on attributes first.

The second approach is to focus on position factors, of which there are twenty-eight. Examples of position factors include analysis, interaction, and leadership. Factors are more difficult to assess but account for 85 percent of why candidates succeed or fail in a particular position.

Sometimes interviewers repeat questions. It's not that they didn't hear your answer the first time; it's just that some questions work in multiple categories. The key is to listen to what the interviewer asks *next*. The probing question that follows the repeat question may suggest what the interviewer was really after.

Preparing for an interview is hard work. There are no shortcuts. Unfortunately, many of you reading this book will be looking for these shortcuts instead of dedicating the time needed in question review and practice to impress the interviewer. The final phase in the job search process, question review and practice, is critical if you want to win in the face-to-face interview. The recommended approach to preparing for an interview is to consider all aspects of the position you are being considered for and what may be required, then review questions listed in both the Position Attributes and Position Factors sections.

For example, consider these leadership position attributes:

While standing in front of a mirror, preferably in your interview power suit, ask yourself the questions to see how you come across as you respond to the questions. Are you smiling? Are you alert and engaged? What is your body language saying? The objective of practice and analysis is to prepare you to respond to difficult questions. The mirror provides visual feedback on your facial expressions, body movements, and body position. Rehearsing for the possible difficult questions will enable you to respond to them and the normal questions effortlessly.

Commonly Used Interviewing Questions, Their Hidden Meanings, And A Few Answers

Question: Where would you like to be, career wise, five years from now?

Interpretation: Interviewers want to get a sense of your personal goals, ambition, drive, and direction. At mid-career, they will be listening for responses relevant to their needs.

Consider This: I take my career seriously. I set yearly, monthly, and weekly goals and do my best in achieving them. Once I understand what is expected of me, my focus is achievement.

Question: Tell me about your proudest achievement.

Interpretation: This question, often worded as "significant accomplishment," ranks among the most predictable and important things you'll be asked. Interviewers want to hear how you tackled something big. It is vital you give them an organized, articulate story.

Consider This: My proudest achievement was ---- a tough issue to resolve. The impact financially on the company was ---- not resolving the problem was out of the question. I played the role of ---- in getting to the core issue and pulled together the team. We accomplished the task by working on it 24/7 for three days.

Question: Give me an example of a time when you had to think outside of the box.

Interpretation: This question is interviewer code for gathering information about your innovativeness, creativity, and initiative. Interviewers want to learn about not only a specific creative idea but also how you came up with it and, more importantly, what you did with that insight.

Consider This: I am a creative person. Let me give you an example of my creativeness.

Question: What negative thing would your last boss say about you?

Interpretation: This is another way of asking about your weaknesses and discerning your ability to see yourself as others see you.

Consider This: Nothing, I performed at the best of my abilities. My boss appreciates my willingness to take on tough assignments and accomplish them.

Question: How and what do you define as "success" in your work and personal life?

Interpretation: This question seeks to determine what is really important to you and how high you set the bar in your performance.

Consider This: In both my personal and working life, I strive for excellence. Success is being there for my family and being of value to my employer.

Question: What are your personal standards for performance, and how would you apply these when managing or working with others?

Interpretation: This question is intended to offer insight into how and on what you set your personal standards.

Consider This: No one is perfect; it's the effort one puts into achieving objectives. I set high standards for myself. All employees want to win; they just need direction and a positive role model.

Question: What do you enjoy most about your work?

Interpretation: This is one of those questions you might be asked more than once. The answer points to your research skills (about the role for which you're interviewing), your understanding of yourself, and whether the two are a good fit. The interviewer wants to know whether the position under consideration offers the same attributes as those you seek.

Consider This: I enjoy being challenged and push to learn more. I am excited when given the opportunity to take on a problem others couldn't resolve.

Question: What can you do for us that other candidates can't?

Interpretation: Some interview questions are more important than others. This is one of the more important ones. It's another way of asking, "Why should I hire you?"

Consider This: I am a builder, problem solver, as well as a motivator of people: not all candidates can handle all three responsibilities.

Question: What specifically interests you about this job/our company?

Interpretation: This question is an indicator of what sort of research, if any, you did on the company and the position.

Consider This: The reputation of the company and its management is important to me. Your company has a reputation for developing talent and I want to be in that type of environment.

Question: If you had to defend a proposal to a group, how would you organize your persuasive presentation?

Interpretation: Your answer indicates how you prepare for an encounter and whether you have experienced this issue before.

Consider This: First, I would make sure I understand whom I am defending the proposal against and what their objectives are and then try to address each objection in my presentation.

101

Question: To what lengths would you go to get a job done?

Interpretation: This is a loaded question. It seeks to understand your limits: how far you'd press yourself, and presumably others, to achieve an objective, as well as how far you'd allow yourself to be pushed.

Consider This: A good question: I am driven to achieving objectives in any form. Working 24/7 is a part of achieving objectives and that is my nature.

Question: Describe your last performance review to me. What were some of the things your boss praised and criticized?

Interpretation: The interviewer is listening for positive information concerning leadership and problem solving, as well as weaknesses to be improved upon. Be honest, nobody's perfect.

Consider This: I was rated ---- by my manager. He/she considers me a top performer. I closed ---- accounts in record time, surprising him/her. He really hasn't criticized me. If I were to criticize myself, I would mention not taking the time to get all the information before charging off.

Question: Give me an example of a project you worked on that had a deadline and how that project turned out.

Interpretation: This is a great opportunity for you, as a strong candidate, to discuss your strengths and how applying them yielded positive results for the company. Remember to be concise and ask the interviewer, at the end of your concise answer, whether he or she wants additional detail.

Consider This: All projects have a short timeline. My example would be —had a financial impact on the bottom line and high visibility. I worked around the clock to get it completed and did in record time.

Question: How would you handle it if you were working on a group project and a peer disagreed with the way you planned to complete your portion of the work?

Interpretation: This question speaks to both your problem-solving skills as well as your diplomatic skills.

Consider This: I would speak with the peer to learn why he or she was in disagreement and explain my approach. If the peer still disagreed with my approach, I would recommend a group discussion to discuss my approach to get buy-in from the group.

Question: How would you handle a situation in which a project you have been working on is in danger of being scrapped by your boss?

Interpretation: Your answer to this question highlights how you respond to unexpected surprises. Sometimes it's not up to your boss, but your boss's boss to determine which projects move forward or get scrapped. Sometimes you have to help your boss convince his or her boss.

Consider This: I would meet with the boss to understand the issues and offer my support and ideas to resolve the problems that have put the project at risk.

Question: What do you admire most about the company you worked for last?

Interpretation: Because no job is forever, every interviewer knows that if you are hired for this position today, you will eventually leave. Therefore, how you answer this question today is a good indicator of how you will answer the question when you seek to leave this company's employment as well. Speak positively about the company and its management. The typical follow-up question will likely be, "Why are you leaving if the company is as great as you say it is?" The response should always be related to slow advancement and lack of challenge, not to anything negative about the company.

Consider This: I really enjoy my company and its management. There is always a time when the job is not challenging and I need to feel there is something more to learn and grow.

Question: What do you think is the most important thing about making a group presentation?

Interpretation: This question addresses daily working life.

Most candidates will need to make presentations to internal and possibly external groups. These settings can be stressful. The answer will indicate how you prepare yourself and how you react to neutralize stress.

Consider This: Making the information easy to understand, starting with an overview and outline and then moving forward methodically, section by section, with frequent circle-backs to ensure the group's understanding.

Question: How much freedom do you feel you need in order to do a job right? Tell me about a situation where you didn't have it. What did you do?

Interpretation: Most companies don't give new hires a great deal of freedom. This question seeks to understand how you will respond to being tightly reined and controlled until you have earned your freedom.

Consider This: I assume you are recruiting independent people who once they understand the objectives, achieve them. Every position I have held started off with oversight and then I was encouraged to use my own expertise to improve the process. I expect to have to prove myself worthy of trust and am fully prepared to do so.

Question: What is important to you in a company, a great work environment, a work group, a boss? Which is most important?

Interpretation: This question seeks to understand how you might fit in the company from a personality perspective.

Consider This: All three are important, though one may be more important than others on any given day. Great products, having fun, being a part of a challenging work group, and working for a boss you can respect and learn from are all important to you.

Question: If you could teach a young protégé one thing, what would it be?

Interpretation: Even if you are not interviewing for a position in which you will have a staff, others will likely look to you for guidance. If you are a senior candidate, those who look to you will probably be younger. Try to ignore the obvious age-related answer.

Consider This: Patience. New workers feel they have to be in the spotlight to get ahead instead of watching and learning how things work before initiating change or volunteering input.

Position Attributes

Alertness

Alertness is the ability to be attentive to all aspects of the environment while working. Alertness involves monitoring one's environment during routine activities.

Question: When and under what circumstances have you "tuned out" in a conversation?

Interpretation: The interviewer is looking for your awareness of poor listening habits. He or she is trying to determine whether you monitor your own inattentiveness in conversations and whether you have a specific strategy for improving your own listening effectiveness.

Consider This: I really never "tune out" of a conversation because there is always something I need to be updated on. If the message is one that is being repeated by the same person I may not be as focused.

Question: Most of us have experienced being more controlled by our environment than by our own career plans. Have you faced such a situation? How did you handle it?

Interpretation: The interviewer is attempting to determine whether the individual is alert to social or political forces in the working environment. Are you the type of individual who is alert to opportunity?

Consider This: I really haven't been in an environment

that didn't have some political undertones. It has never been an issue; performance in the position always provided the next opportunity.

Question: Describe a situation in which you observed conflict that existed between two members of higher management. How did the conflict affect you? How did you react to it?

Interpretation: The interviewer is trying to determine if you are able to gauge your actions in light of the interpersonal environment. Were you able to be thorough in describing the events or behavior of others? Obviously, since the interviewer was not present during these events, his or her interpretation of your answer will be gauged, to a significant degree, by how you answer rather than by what you answer.

Consider This: When upper management is in conflict the best direction is to focus on the objectives and not be pulled into the issue. Win respect from management for staying focused on the goals.

Question: When have your subordinates kept you in the dark about their performance?

Interpretation: The interviewer is trying to assess whether you are aware that information may have been hidden from you. Evaluating your awareness through a specific example of how subordinates can cover up mistakes tends to be a good approach.

Consider This: I cannot recall ever not being on top of my subordinates' performance.

Question: How did you monitor the performance of subordinates in your last position?

Interpretation: The interviewer is trying to determine if you had a specific method for evaluating subordinate performance; most companies have standard methods but some companies allow flexibility. The interviewer will be interested in observing whether you are able to give specific examples rather than simply relying on personality or trait judgments.

Consider This: All of my subordinates have objectives that are discussed with them on a biweekly basis. Each one had achievable milestones that are tracked and corrections made when necessary.

Question: What is your procedure for keeping track of matters that require your constant attention? When has your system broken down?

Interpretation: Do you utilize a reminder system—a specific procedure, an assistant—for maintaining awareness of important details? In today's economy, free technologies, such as reminders on an electronic calendar or even a whiteboard scheduler, are good options.

Consider This: With the tools available today there is no excuse for not being on top of everything in your business sector. Avail yourself of every possible tool that will increase your efficiency.

Question: In terms of dollars and cents, what is the costliest mistake (or near mistake) you've ever made? How much could a poor decision on your part cost your employer?

Interpretation: Like the question about the past predicting future changes, this question seeks to evaluate the extent to which you are sensitive to situations. In this case, it's a question of whether you are aware of the costs of a poor decision. The interviewer is looking for your ability to estimate a specific dollar amount associated with a decision-making error.

Question: What has been your biggest mistake in employee selection? Do you now understand why the mistake was made?

Interpretation: The interviewer is looking to determine your ability to self-criticize, be alert to, and profit from selection mistakes. Can you comment on how you benefited from the experience?

Consider This: Your mistake was getting off your interview plan and losing control of the interview. You now script out what you want to accomplish and stick to it.

Question: In your most recent position, what business- or process-related problems have you identified that previously had been overlooked?

Interpretation: The interviewer is trying to ascertain how much effort you made or needed to make to identify problems and what impact your identification of those problems had on the department or company.

Consider This: There were several, the major one was —I discovered it and took it on to solve it, which I did in the first ---- days in the position.

Question: What aspects of your work do you consider most crucial?

Interpretation: The interviewer is looking for your grasp of functional responsibilities. He or she may be trying to determine where and how your time is spent.

Consider This: Your ability to stay cool under pressure and stay focused on the objective is how you continuously get the job done.

Ambiguity

Ambiguity is the quality of being in doubt, uncertain, obscure, or indistinct.

Interpretation: The ambiguous work environment may have shifting priorities, vague deadlines, and unpredictable or varying hierarchy. If the ability to succeed in work assignments depends on the ability to cope with uncertainty, obscure or indistinct work parameters, and unpredictable working conditions, this important question will be a signal of this need.

Consider This: Rarely do you have all the information you need to make a decision. This is where experience comes in and helps narrow the choices.

Question: Do you prefer to have a job in which you have well laid out tasks and responsibilities, or one in which your work changes on a frequent basis?

Interpretation: The job is not going to change for you. The intent of this question is to determine whether your preference for structured, as opposed to non-structured work, fits the current opportunity. Depending on your answer, the interviewer may probe further into the areas of flexibility in working in an unstructured situation.

Consider This: You have worked in both types of organizations. You prefer the constantly changing organization because it provides more of a challenge and better use of your skill set.

Question: Describe a time when it was necessary for you to postpone making a decision even when you felt frustrated in having to hold back.

Interpretation: With this question, the interviewer is seeking to assess your ability to make good decisions regarding postponed actions while managing your frustration.

Consider This: In answering this question, think of a decision you were ready to make and were delayed in making the decision. It comes across better if it was a financial decision, where taking additional time is sometimes wise. This shows you think through your decisions.

Question: How did you prepare for this interview?

Interpretation: This particular question explores whether and the extent to which you prepared for the interview. List the materials you researched and then ask if additional detail is desired.

Consider This: This is a critical test of your interest in the position. Your response should be you have researched the company and management team, as well as some of the issues facing the company. Note: The follow-up question then may be what are the issues?

Question: Describe for me one or two areas on which you and your manager disagreed.

Interpretation: Like many of the previous questions, this one seeks to assess your self-assessment skills and whether, what, and how you have learned from your assessments of yourself. How you handled disagreements in the past portends how you will handle them in the future with your next superior.

Consider This: The correct answer is you and your manager agree on most issues and when you don't you meet and discuss the issues and come to a decision.

Question: When would you say that your technical knowledge in ---- was put to best use in discovering the causes of a problem that had baffled others?

Interpretation: This question seeks to determine whether you are able to integrate technical knowledge and practical elements of a problem situation into a meaningful solution. Your answer, as always, should be specific and brief, and end with a question about whether the interviewer desires additional detail.

Consider This: This is the opportunity to address your skill expertise in a real situation; focus on the difficulty of the problem to be solved and your approach to solving it.

Question: What are your most significant strengths that you would bring to this position?

Interpretation: This question seeks to assess your understanding of your strengths. Assuming you have done your homework and know both your strengths and the position's needs, this question provides a great opportunity to speak to your strengths and match them to the position. Is there a match? If so, say so loud and clear. Don't leave it up to the interviewer to understand and interpret a self-deprecating answer.

Consider This: The answer to this question is similar to the above question with the exception that this is where you mention all four of your strengths you bring to the position. In a previous section we discussed only offering four strengths to better focus your candidacy.

Question: What could you do for us that someone else could not do?

Interpreter: This question is, in essence, a rephrasing of the previous question. It seeks to understand whether you know your strengths and the needs of the position.

Consider This: What you bring is motivation, new ideas, high energy, and a package of skills.

Question: What control of financial data would you want and why?

Interpretation: These days, maintaining tight control of the bottom line is vitally important. Whether that control requires intimate knowledge of the company's financial data or requires knowledge of external data may be different for each possible opportunity. Regardless of the source and nature of the financial data, this question seeks to understand what level of control you perceive you want or need.

Consider This: If you are responsible for the financial results, you need to have the full responsibilities and accountability. If it is shared, where is the accountability?

Analysis

Analysis involves the separation of the whole into its component parts so as to conduct an examination of a complex problem, its elements, and their relationship. Do you demonstrate an ability and willingness to separate the whole into its component parts? Can you make fine discriminations and deal with complex problems? Can you evaluate and make sound judgments? Your answers to these questions lead the interviewer to make these conclusions about you.

Question: What is your definition of analysis? Give an example of what you feel was your best analysis of a business situation.
Interpretation: This question seeks to help the interviewer determine whether you understand how to break down a

problem. Does the example given show an ability to deal with complex decisions? Remember to be precise and concise, then offer to provide details if the interviewer desires them.

Question: Describe a technical problem you solved on your last job that would shed light on your analytical ability.

Interpretation: This question seeks to determine if you can describe a specific problem that was solved. The interviewer gauges your answer by whether and how well you can describe the key elements of the problem and/or the logic of the solution.

Consider This: Another opportunity to shine, this answer should be rehearsed in advance. The example needs to be one that had financial impact on the organization.

Question: What have been major obstacles which you have had to overcome on your past job? How did you deal with them?

Interpretation: Your answer to this question helps the interviewer assess your awareness of obstacles and the use of specific approaches for the solution of problems.

Consider This: The answer needs to address work issues, not personal issues involving other employees or management.

Question: Sooner or later, everybody makes mistakes. What was the most significant mistake you made on your last job and explain why you made it?

Interpretation: Like many other questions, this one seeks to assess your level of self-assessment and capacity to correct flaws in your behavior. Your answer also helps the interviewer to understand how you define the actual significance of the error and whether you can objectively dissect the reasons for the mistake.

Consider This: In answering this question, pick a mistake that is understandable and had no financial impact on the organization.

Question: Describe the most risky business decision you have made. How did you go about it? How did it work out?

Interpretation: This question seeks to determine your awareness of the risks involved in decision making. The interviewer is looking for hints as to whether you are willing to make decisions in a risky environment or if your approach is more cautious. The rightness or wrongness of your answer depends on the cultural climate of the organization. If you've done your homework and your honest answer matches the organization's needs, the interview will move forward.

Consider This: Relate the decision to something that has an impact on the organization, and make sure that you mention that you researched and consulted others before making the decision.

Question: In what areas does your current decision-making responsibility create risks for your employer? When have you been most acutely aware of the risks?

Interpretation: This question seeks to determine your awareness of the potential consequences of poor decision making and how successfully you have mitigated those risks.

Consider This: The answer has to show your maturity in assessing the risk/reward process in making a risky decision.

Question: Have you ever worked in an environment that was characterized by frequent crises or emergencies? Why did frequent crisis situations occur? How did you handle them?

Interpretation: Some companies just seem to operate in perpetual crisis mode. Sometimes there's a reason for it, sometimes not. By asking you this question, your interviewer is trying to determine whether you were aware of the causes of the crisis/emergency situations. Were measures taken that effectively dealt with the problem? If not, why not?

Consider This: The answer to this is no, you have worked in organizations that head off crisis situations by staying in front of the issues. If you state you have had experience in crisis situations on a continuing basis, the interviewer may question your role in the organization.

Question: Provide an example of how you make judgments when faced with a difficult problem.

Interpretation: The interviewer is listening for the voice of a detective in your answer to this question. Demonstrate your capacity to think through the problem rather than react to it.

Consider This: The answer has to be how you approach and think through problems in detail.

Question: Can you give me an example of what you term as a complex problem in your position?

Interpretation: This is an opportunity for you to distinguish between a complex problem and a difficult problem. What makes the complex problem complex?

Consider This: A complex problem requires several levels of input to resolve, normally beyond your level.

Question: Tell me about an event that really challenged you. How did you meet the challenge? In what way was your approach different from that of others?

Interpretation: This question seeks to identify your skill at comparing yourself to others, assessing your response to challenges, being aware of the downside or financial impact of failure, and how and why your approach was unique.

Consider This: Interviewers want to know what your limits are when facing a challenge. Your example needs to cover your well thought through analysis and action plan.

Question: Describe to me how your job relates to the overall goals of your department and company.

Interpretation: This question allows you to connect yourself to the organization. Anyone who does not understand how he or she contributes to the company is going to be less concerned for the good of the company.

Consider This: Your answer needs to lay out the organization structure and where your position contributes to its success. The kiss of death in an interview is not being able to explain how the pieces go together in explaining where you fit.

Question: Growing companies sometimes have difficulty in responding to potential customers' demands. How do you define which potential customers to direct your attention to?

Interpretation: Your answer to this question helps the interviewer assess whether you have a systematic approach to defining which customers are the most important. If you've done your homework, you should be able to relate your answer to the company's values.

Consider This: All customers are valuable. Some customers mean more to the future growth of your company. Maintaining customers is critical, but some relationships cannot be expanded, so new customers must be developed.

Assertiveness

Assertiveness is the quality of stating or declaring positively with force or vigor. It implies stating confidently without a need for proof or regard for evidence. The candidate who demonstrates this ability makes his or her position known by his or her very presence. Assertiveness isn't always a good thing. The interviewer must assess whether the assertive candidate can take an adversarial position, challenge, or work with hard-to-please or difficult people, and how the candidate attempts to challenge, influence, or persuade others.

Question: You are in a meeting with several high-level managers. They strongly advocate embarking on a new strategy that you do not believe will be successful. What do you do?

Interpretation: This question seeks to uncover whether you voice opposition and strive to change minds, or go along with the management. Your answer might be right or wrong, depending on the position for which you are applying, the temperaments of your potential peers and superiors, and the overall climate of the organization. If you've done your homework, you should be able to answer honestly and still be correct.

Consider This: Whether you speak up depends on the role you play in the decision. If you are responsible for its success, you need to address the issues not covered by the senior managers. In this situation, challenging sets up a power play. Presenting

115

information and expanding their knowledge of the issue always wins and saves face.

Question: Tell me about how you have handled a talkative customer. How did you ensure that you were communicating effectively with him/her?

Interpretation: This question could be referring to an internal customer or an external customer. In most cases, the interviewer is seeking to determine whether you prefer to communicate orally or in written format to emphasize points.

Question: Please give me a few examples of what you consider being assertive in business situations.

Interpretation: The interviewer will use your response to gauge whether your definition of assertiveness was over the top or applied professionally. Again, this may be a case of corporate culture.

Consider This: Being assertive is a double-edged sword to be used against you. What the interviewer is listening for is your not backing away but taking a stand.

Question: Describe a situation in which one of your decisions was challenged by higher management. How did you react?

Interpretation: Like many other questions highlighted here, part of the answer is in your delivery of the answer. Be concise and precise. The interviewer will be listening for whether you are able to maturely emphasize and explain the rationale for your decision, rather than indicating acquiescence to authority.

Question: Describe a situation in which you communicated some unpleasant feelings to a supervisor. What happened?

Interpretation: The interviewer will be assessing your body language and tone, as well as your words, when you answer this question. Were you comfortable in confronting the supervisor? Are you able to keep your feelings in check now (and were you then)? Was the communication hostile and aggressive or mature and assertive?

Question: Describe a time when you had to sell an idea in difficult circumstances.

Interpretation: This question seeks to uncover your skill and experience with persuasion in difficult situations and evaluates your effectiveness in changing the opinions of others. The interviewer will attempt to determine whether you gave up too quickly or persisted too long.

Consider This: This is the opportunity to impress the interviewer with your ability to persuade others, the higher level the better.

Question: How do your current coworkers describe you—as being more fun-loving and happy-go-lucky, or as being more reserved and quiet? How does this affect your ability to communicate an unpopular opinion?

Interpretation: This question seeks to identify the extent to which you are able to speak up and command the attention of your peers and supervisors.

Consider This: Employers want individuals who fit into their organization. In responding to this question, consider the type of environment of the position; every company is different.

Question: When have you been told that you were too pushy/too nice? What did you do to be told that?

Interpretation: This question seeks to determine whether you are aware of how others perceive your behavior and whether your pushiness or niceness interfered with your ability to do the job. Are you pushy, or are you nice? How, if at all, did you use that feedback to change your behavior? Did you agree with the description of your approach as having been pushy or nice?

Consider This: In responding to this question, it may be better to state you have never been asked this question, but if you were, you would say you are always fair but firm.

Question: What's the "gutsiest" thing you've ever said or done?

Interpretation: This question seeks to address whether you

feel comfortable in an assertive role. What kind of circumstances elicited the assertiveness? Your answer will need to match the company's culture in order for you to fit well in the company.

Consider This: Gutsiest means you stuck your neck out. In responding to the question make sure your example is business related and had a successful outcome. Never give an answer that leaves you in a bad light.

Question: Do you challenge people more than you should? When have you been told you are too aggressive?

Interpretation: This question seeks to identify your definition of aggressive behavior and asks for examples of when you demonstrated it. Again, this question points to how you might fit in the company culture.

Consider This: The right answer may be that you always challenge your employees because it keeps them sharp and highly motivated. The right employees want to be challenged and appreciated for their efforts.

Question: Explain the techniques you might use to overcome the objections of others.

Interpretation: This question seeks to determine whether and how you can formulate consensus to win over others who pose objections. In a corporate setting, there are always those who advocate for whatever you're not promoting.

Consider This: To overcome objections requires give on both sides. Understanding the other person's reasoning provides the necessary information to address each objection.

Question: Give me an example from your current job that demonstrates your persistence.

Interpretation: This question seeks to identify your definition of persistence. Like many other questions of this nature, your answer is a clue to whether and how well you would fit in the company culture.

Consider This: Persistence is never giving up while exploring other avenues to achieve your objective. It is not confronting others until they acquiesce.

Question: What techniques do you use when you are required to challenge the ideas of others?

Interpretation: If you guessed this was another of those company-fit questions, you were right. The objective of this question is to determine whether you take a confrontational approach or a persuasive one.

Attentiveness

Attentiveness is the ability to pay attention to details and tasks. Attentive people are able to be observant and maintain their concentration, even in the midst of distractions and other demands.

Breadth

Breadth is exemplified by a comprehensive understanding of functional role responsibilities. Individuals who demonstrate breadth are capable of seeing both sides of situations and maintaining the appropriate perspective on problems.

Question: What would you say are the major qualities this position demands?

Interpretation: This question seeks to understand your level of awareness that every job has its good and bad points and every job demands certain qualities and excludes others. Your answer must prove you understand what the job entails.

Consider This: This is the opportunity to display your research information on the position and company.

Question: What would you say are the broad-based responsibilities of your current (last) job?

Interpretation: This is a variation on the theme of the previous question. This particular question views your role and limits of responsibility from your own perspective and that of others. Your answer speaks to how you will fit in this organization's corporate hierarchy.

Coping

Coping is the ability to deal with and overcome problems, differences, or difficulties. The candidate with good coping skills demonstrates the ability to handle stress and maintain flexibility with others. He or she can deal with time pressures, changing demands, or inflexible work schedules.

Question: Give an example of what you consider stress in your position.

Interpretation: This question speaks to how you will handle the expected stress in the position. If you have done your homework, you will know how much and what kind of stress you will likely encounter in this position.

Consider This: Make sure your example is impressive; a response that reflects a stress level below what the position requires could end your candidacy.

Question: How do you help your managers and employees handle stress?

Interpretation: If you are a candidate for a management role, your answer should address your interaction with your team and focus on coping skills you impart or demonstrate. If you have developed techniques to help your team manage stress, now is the time to mention them. Be concise and specific and then ask if additional details are desired.

Question: Give an example of a situation in which you hung in there to achieve a business objective.

Interpretation: Regardless of how you managed to hang in there, it is safe to assume the business objective was worth the effort, if only because it was a corporate objective and not your own personal agenda. Focus on the business aspects.

Consider This: In selecting an example, make sure you include how you were rewarded or recognized for your effort. By leaving out this important point, or if there was no recognition for your effort, you diminish the importance of the effort.

Question: Customers frequently create a great deal of pressure. What has been your experience in this area?

Interpretation: Every position faces customers, whether they're internal ones or external ones. This question is meant to evaluate your depth and level of experience in coping with customer complaints and anger. It is specifically meant to evaluate if you were able to cope with such pressures over a significant period of time. Were your coping mechanisms effective?

Consider This: Use an example of when you were faced by an upset individual and turned the situation around to your favor.

Question: What type of pressures do you currently feel on your job? How do you cope with these pressures?

Interpretation: Your answer to these questions identifies the extent of the pressure in your current position and points to your ability to work comfortably and effectively under that kind of pressure. Do you maintain active involvement or retreat from the situation?

Question: What types of things make you angry? How do you react in these situations?

Interpretation: Your answer to these questions is meant to determine whether you have a quick temper. How you answer is as important as what you say; since your answer signals whether you can conceal hostile feelings to avoid creating social conflict.

Consider This: Never admit you get angry; instead state you may get irritated but you never lose your smile.

121

Question: How do you react when you see coworkers disagreeing? Do you get involved or hold back?

Interpretation: This question points to your possible role as a mediator in interpersonal conflict. Companies are always looking for people to fill this role. If you are able to maintain a sense of calm when others are in disagreement, you may be just what the company was looking for.

Consider This: The answer to this question is that you are a natural mediator who is often sought out because you take the time to listen to all parties. You have discovered that you do not have to give a response, because most of the time after airing out the issue the parties resolve the issue between themselves.

Question: Have you ever been fired?

Interpretation: Being fired is traumatic, but it can also be a learning experience. Don't lie. Your answer is a signal of how you cope with trauma.

Consider This: In a way being fired, especially in your early years, is considered a positive as long as it is not for a criminal act.

Question: Characterize the individuals with whom you have had the greatest difficulty working and why.

Interpretation: If you haven't had great success working with Type A personalities in the past, you will likely experience similar non-success in the future. You may not know whether the types of people with whom you have difficulty working are present in large numbers at the company, but your interviewer probably does. You need to know yourself and the company's composition in order to answer this question well.

Consider This: Startup companies hire A types because of the high risk taking that requires a 24/7 personality; if you are not a risk taker and only want to work a forty-hour week, target only established companies.

Question: When I contact your past managers, what examples are they going to use to demonstrate your ability to hang in there to achieve your objectives?

Interpretation: The interviewer is looking for your ability to persevere in accomplishing objectives in the face of obstacles or discouragement.

Consider This: Even if you are not asked this question, bring it up in the interview to showcase your major accomplishments.

Creativity

Creativity is the ability to produce results through the application of imaginative skill. The ideal candidate, regardless of the role or position, demonstrates the ability to innovate and be creative. He or she can develop ideas and deal with new concepts effectively.

Question: Give me your best example of when you used your creative talents to solve a business-related problem.

Interpretation: This is probably your best opportunity to demonstrate your creativity.

Question: In regard to marketing and sales, have you ever been told you were a creative person? Describe the circumstances.

Interpretation: You are all but guaranteed to hear this question if you are interviewing for a position in this capacity. Even if you're not directly responsible for sales and marketing, you will likely be called upon to contribute. Do you think you're a creative person? Does your example support your claim of being creative?

Consider This: As part of your preparation for the interview, rehearse this answer so it comes off sounding natural. If the creative example is not impressive and not related to the position you are applying for, the interview may be over.

Question: What must you do that you consider being your biggest time-waster at work? How would you change it if you could?

Interpretation: The most frequent (and true) response to this type of question is meetings. The interviewer is trying to determine if you have a method for creatively reducing the time wasted in meetings, group idea exchange sessions, and so on. If you answer poorly, the interviewer will likely reevaluate your answer to the questions regarding creativity in a less enthusiastic manner.

Question: What three things have you done that you are the most proud of and why?

Interpretation: The interpreter will be listening to ascertain whether your accomplishments are business-related or personal. Ideally, your answer should be business-related, unless you've succeeded in scaling Mount Everest or winning a marathon.

Consider This: This is a simple question that will fall flat unless the three things relate to work accomplishments.

Question: As a young person, what types of activities were you involved in that would help you develop creative skills? Be specific.

Interpretation: This is a sort of open-ended question that some companies like to throw into an interview. If you are asked this question, your interviewer will observe whether and how you detail creativity-building experiences during youth. The assumption is that if you were creative in your youth, you are still creative now.

Question: What would you regard as being the most creative activity you have engaged in? Did it bring you recognition, financial reward, or personal satisfaction?

Interpretation: This question seeks to identify whether you can be specific with regard to a creative accomplishment. The interviewer will observe whether the focus of your accomplishment is associated with the creative act itself or with the results of the act.

Question: What would you observe to be the most creative bit of work done in your field in the last few years? How has the work had an impact on you?

Interpretation: This question is meant to determine whether and how you can describe creative work. It also helps the interviewer to assess your creative appreciation and whether and how it has had an impact on personal self-development.

Consider This: This question is also probing whether you stay current with what is going on in your field.

Question: Do you think everyone has the capacity to be creative? What experiences lead you to your conclusions?

Interpretation: Your answer is an indicator of whether you have a theory of creativity. Is it seen as a gift or as something that can be developed? In the position under consideration, will you be expected to deliver creativity or nurture it in certain employees? If you have done your homework, this question should be easy to answer.

Question: What's the most creative thing you've ever done outside of your work?

Interpretation: This question allows you to offer insight into how you see the application of creativity to everyday problems and not just to "works of art."

Consider This: This is where you detail events outside the work environment; otherwise always focus on work-related activities.

Decision Making

Decision making involves the ability to analyze, understand, and reason, combined with the capacity and willingness to make sound decisions. There are two central issues in decision making: the experience and capacity to analyze, understand, and reason, and the capacity and willingness to risk the consequences of making an incorrect decision.

Question: Thus far in your career, can you think of one business situation or problem that almost overwhelmed you? What was it? How did you handle it?

Interpretation: Most candidates will not freely give a situation in which they almost lost control. Be prepared to answer this question and do so honestly. It shows integrity, strength of character, and your preparedness.

Consider This: In answering this question, describe the magnitude of the problem and its possible impact, then the steps you took to resolve it and the recognition you received from your superiors.

Question: In your current or most recent position, cite an example of the types of decisions you make or made without consulting the president. What is or was your level of authority?

Interpretation: Your response to this set of questions is meant to yield insight into the level of decision-making responsibility you are accustomed to handling. If the position for which you are interviewing has a different (particularly lower) level of authority and responsibility, will that be a problem?

Consider This: This is what is called a "leveling question" in that you reveal your true level of authority in the organization, and at times it is asked to check on what you have previously said.

Question: Give an example of a risky business decision that you faced. What approach did you take in making the decision?

Interpretation: The interviewer will try to ascertain, from your example, whether your idea of and approach to risk taking and analysis demonstrate a mature approach to a decision or a shoot-from-the-hip approach. Does the approach fit into the operating style of the president at this new organization? Your homework should have prepared you to answer this question.

Question: What one work-related business decision would you rethink, if you had the opportunity to do so? What would you do differently?

Interpretation: This is another of those what-you-say and how-you-say-it questions. The interviewer is listening for the decision-making process involved. Did you use all the tools and information available before reaching a decision?

Consider This: Everyone has made decisions that in hindsight, they would change. This shows you are capable of making decisions and reassessing the results to improve yourself.

Question: What was the most unpopular decision you had to make?

Interpretation: Decisions that involve managing a financial impact on the company are of the greatest interest to most companies. Be sure you cite a positive outcome or are prepared to explain if that was not the case.

Consider This: Many people cite human resources issues in response to this question; try to remain focused on business issues.

Question: Have you ever had to tell a subordinate that his or her performance is not up to par? How did you handle it?

Interpretation: This question is intended to determine your ability to distinguish and deliver specific performance information prior to moving into a difficult performance communication. Be sure your answer focuses on work behaviors rather than personality.

Consider This: The best response is to use as an example how you turned around the performance of an employee.

Decisiveness

Decisiveness is the ability to deal with and overcome problems, differences, or difficulties and having the power and ability to make on-the-spot decisions to represent management in a self-assured manner. The decisive individual can arrive at a solution that ends uncertainly and influences a sound business outcome. Do you, as a candidate, demonstrate the ability to handle stress and maintain flexibility with others? Can you deal with time pressures, changing demands, or unpredictable work schedules? Do you as a candidate demonstrate the ability to make sound, on-the-spot decisions? Can you clarify uncertainty and influence the outcome of future events?

Question: In your current or most recent position, what types of decisions do you make without consulting your immediate supervisor?

Interpretation: This question is intended to identify your awareness of the boundaries of decision-making authority. Are you willing to take charge if necessary?

Consider This: Make sure the decisions you use in this example illustrate your leadership and its financial impact on the organization.

Question: Tell me about a situation in which you have had to stand firm on a decision you made, even though it made you unpopular.

Interpretation: This question is meant to demonstrate whether your stand resulted from stubbornness or commitment. Companies need managers and staff members who can balance stubbornness and commitment with sufficient flexibility to work well in a team setting.

Consider This: Your answer needs to indicate you have enough expertise and knowledge to stick with the decision, not just that you want to be right.

Question: Describe a time when you were under pressure to make a decision. Did you react immediately or take your time in deciding what to do?

Interpretation: This question seeks to assess whether you are impulsive and reactive to pressure or whether you momentarily retreat to logically analyze and evaluate options. Be aware that, while the reactive, quick-coping style may be desirable in certain jobs, the more analytical and methodical style may be valuable in other types of positions. Your homework should enable you to answer well.

Consider This: Above all you must convey that you keep a

cool head when facing pressure to make a decision.

Question: Can you describe a situation in which you have found it important to take a stand, even when the outcome would likely be detrimental to you?

Interpretation: Your answer to this question points to your willingness to assume a firm position and whether that decision is an indication of high integrity or inflexibility. Does the position you describe appear to warrant your having taken a firm position?

Consider This: Being able to be decisive even in political times is a mark of a leader who is focused on what's best for the organization.

Question: In what types of situations do you think it is important for a manager to use democratic/participative techniques in making decisions as opposed to making unilateral decisions?

Interpretation: Interviewers ask this question to observe whether you have awareness of participative management techniques. The answer to this question may also yield insight into the extent to which you can be flexible in using either authoritative or democratic approaches to decision making.

Consider This: Organizations expect managers to be both democratic and participative; not to do so indicates maverick behavior, which is normally short lived.

Question: Describe a situation in which you changed your mind, even after you publicly committed to a particular idea.

Interpretation: Your answer to this question is a clue into what sorts of issues you find to be important and the situations under which you were willing to change your stance. Were you motivated to change your position because of new information or because of social pressures?

Question: As a manager, have you ever had to fire anyone? If so, what were the circumstances and how did you handle it?

Interpretation: Nobody enjoys firing people, but sometimes

it has to be done. Did you take charge of the situation at an early point or let the problem exist over a period of time? Offer a concise, precise answer.

Consider This: If you have never had to fire an employee, you may not be experienced enough for the position.

Question: Tell me about your early life, what things made you happy and unhappy? What influence did your father play in your success in your early life?

Interpretation: While you might think this to be an awkward question (and it can be), the answer can also be very telling. It yields insight into the level of success your parents had in their careers, and colors your perception of career success. Most people outdo their parents by one position.

Consider This: Always make this answer as positive as possible; a dysfunctional early life may be interpreted as carrying some baggage over into one's later life.

Question: Tell me about your value system. How was it developed?

Interpretation: Similar to the question about your father's career, this set of questions points to the role your parents and siblings played in the development of your value system. It's a challenge to keep this answer short and sweet, but make a diligent effort to do so.

Consider This: What is really being asked for is information on your family; this is difficult to get in the normal questioning process.

Function

Function is the ability to perform in a position with adaptation to the structure or designs of the position and/or organization. Individuals who can function well are respected and promoted.

Question: What are your five highest skills, in order of importance?

Interpretation: This question seeks to understand not only your five highest skills but whether you understand enough about the position for which you are interviewing to relate them to the needs of that position.

Consider This: These five skills need to be on the tip of your tongue to be believable, and focus on the interviewer's face when answering the question for impact.

Question: What have you done that helped increase sales or profits? How did you go about it?

Interpretation: Even if you don't have primary responsibility for increasing sales or profits, you should have the ability to relate to bottom-line responsibility.

Consider This: How does your job affect the bottom line?

Question: Describe your ideal position.

Interpretation: This question is meant, in part, to assess whether you did your homework. Does the position offered match your ideal position? Are the skill requirements those you currently possess and enjoy using?

Consider This: The perfect job is the one you are interviewing for at that moment; relate the fit of your skills to the position needs.

Question: What would you change about your current position? What aspects do you like least?

Interpretation: This question seeks to determine whether the things you would change and least like are part of the position for which you are under consideration. Your needs and preferences will either match or not. If you don't like to do something that's critical to this position, you're not a match, regardless of your qualifications. Make sure you do your homework before you are presented with this question!

Consider This: Is there enough challenge or opportunity to introduce new ideas to improve the organization in the job for which you are interviewing?

Question: What are you looking for in your next position?

Interpretation: This question is meant to examine your desires and the company's ability to provide them. The chances of maintaining a long-term working relationship lessen as the number of desires the company is unable or unwilling to provide increases. If you did your homework, you should be able to answer both honestly and convincingly.

Consider This: The chance to innovate and learn new things and be allowed to exceed expectations is what you are seeking in your next position.

Question: What are the three most important responsibilities in your current or most recent position? What special skills or knowledge do or did you need in order to perform these duties?

Interpretation: Your answers to this set of questions yield insight into your functional background and the depth of understanding you possess. Ideally, your answers should parallel the needs of the position for which you are interviewing.

Consider This: Goal achievement, staff management, and innovation

Question: What achievements are you most proud of in your current or most recent position?

Interpretation: You may think this question is your opportunity to crow. It's not. Your achievements should be career-related and demonstrate true benefits to your department and the company. Ideally, these same benefits should match the needs of the position for which you are interviewing.

Consider This: Your team is a winner and you are known as a talent developer.

Question: What was the most important project you have worked on at your current or most recent position?

Interpretation: Your answer to this question points to your functional fit and how you define importance. Your answer should revolve around the company, not personal satisfaction.

Consider This: Think financial impact and contribution to the overall success of the company.

Question: How have you remained current in your field?

Interpretation: This question addresses whether you have a realistic approach and method to staying current, as well as whether you follow up on your plans.

Consider This: The best employees are those who understand the strategic need to keep abreast of what is going on in their field and are not surprised with new advancements. They plan for these changes.

Question: What factors would you say account for your career success to date and what are your future career plans?

Interpretation: In your answer to this question, the interviewer is listening for your individual success factors and aspirations. Are they within the company's ability to provide or at least offer them?

Consider This: Staying in the forefront of change and building great teams and leaders.

Question: What concerns (based on the information provided to date) do you have about this position?

Interpretation: This is your opportunity to prove you have listened to what's been told to you and what you've found out on your own through your research. Ask intelligent questions.

Goal Setting

Goal setting is the ability to define goals, set target dates, manage and prioritize objectives, establish performance standards, and evaluate results. Do you demonstrate the ability to define goals, set target dates, manage and prioritize objectives, establish performance standards, and evaluate results? Does your experience and answers to questions reinforce these abilities?

133

Question: Give an example of how you have organized and accomplished your business objectives.

Interpretation: Your response to this question provides the interviewer with insights into how you view goal setting. He or she is listening for you to mention examples of deliverables.

Consider This: Explain how you establish goals, think them through, and develop a plan to execute them.

Question: What has been your success rate in achieving your applications and projects?

Interpretation: Most candidates will attest to a high achievement in goals accomplishment. The smart interviewer will listen for how they verify it. Don't lie.

Question: In your career thus far, where have you experienced the best examples of goal setting in a business situation? As a manager, give me an example of how you have handled the establishment and accomplishment of business goals?

Interpretation: Your answer points to both your understanding of goal setting and your idea of what good examples of goal setting are. Are the examples you list examples of stretch, or are they easily achieved?

Consider This: Indicate you are always seeking improvements and methods of improving the goal process and then give your best example of a stretch goal.

Question: Which of your stated business objectives were not accomplished in your last position—and why not?

Interpretation: The interviewer is listening for two pieces of information: Was the objective an important one and was the objective well thought out? Of course, he or she is also interested in why you didn't achieve it, so don't skimp on that part of the answer.

Consider This: The common answer is a shift in the economy or target companies fell on hard times. Given this, what did you do to overcome the problem?

Question: What were some of the business objectives you have been given that you thought were a waste of time?

Interpretation: Your response to this question should yield insight into how you view accepting business objectives and which ones you think are important. In addition, your answer is a clue to your attitude when it comes to following orders with which you don't necessarily agree.

Consider This: In responding to this question, make sure the example of a waste of time objective is self-evident.

Question: Looking back on your last position, what would have been a better way to establish, monitor, and accomplish business objectives?

Interpretation: The interviewer who asks this question is listening for your creative ideas, as well as possible problems carrying out objectives in your last position. If you have demonstrated creative ideas in the past, you can do so in the future. Problems, of course, might also be repeated, but it is hoped your preparation will allow you to explain your way around that matter.

Question: Evaluate your past employer in terms of emphasis on goal setting and planning.

Interpretation: Your answer to this question is your opportunity to give specific examples of failure in planning with an eye to how you would have done things differently. Is your description related to the planning process or the objectives? You may not be able to change the objectives in the role for which you are interviewing. Remember: don't speak negatively about a current or prior employer.

Question: Do you engage in personal planning as well as professional? If yes, what are your goals?

Interpretation: This set of questions is intended to yield insight into whether you lead a compartmentalized life and you plan only work-related goals, or whether you are fully organized and consider planning and organization to be natural aspects of

135

your personality.

Consider This: If you do not take your planning skills over into your personal life, chances are you really aren't into goal setting.

Question: In your career, have you ever experienced a serious conflict of goals? Tell me about it. How did you decide which goal was more important?

Interpretation: The interviewer seeks to understand whether the prioritizing of goals was done on a rational basis or an intuitive one. Were the reasons for choosing one goal over another personal or organizational? Who made these decisions?

Consider This: This question is looking for conflicts with your management on direction. As a manager you take direction. Employers want to see if you do as you are told or question if this is the right direction. Some employers want managers who carry out directions without comment.

Question: Do you set short-term as well as long-term goals? Which ones take priority? In other words, will you sacrifice short-term goals like a vacation for long-term goals, like buying a house?

Interpretation: This is a great example of where your homework plays a critical role. Does the job require more emphasis on short-term goals or long-term goals? Is your orientation in line with the job's priorities?

Question: Can you describe a time when you stuck with a goal you'd set, even though now, in retrospect, it was an obvious mistake? In other words, did commitment to a goal ever prevent you from being as flexible as you should have been?

Interpretation: Is it possible for you to commit to a goal and still maintain flexibility? Can you evaluate past performance in a broader perspective than simple goal attainment or nonattainment? Are you capable of questioning the value of a goal? Companies look for people who are flexible and can see beyond their immediate needs.

Consider This: When you realized the goal was a mistake

did you try to adjust it or replace it?

Question: What techniques do you use to define and establish goals for others?

Interpretation: This question relates to whether you have a process for goal setting. There are a variety of possible processes.

Interaction

Interaction is the ability to listen, negotiate, influence, and clarify issues or concepts and gather information. Do you demonstrate the ability to interact well and get along well with others? Can you demonstrate the use of these communication skills essential to success in the business environment?

Question: If we surveyed the individuals who have worked for you over the past five years, how would they rate you on the management skills of leading and interacting with them? In what areas would they suggest improvement, based on their experiences working for you?

Interpretation: This question asks you to focus on a five-year historical period instead of the recent past. The interviewer will likely listen for some evolution or change in your management style over this period of time.

Consider This: In responding to this question any revelation of an improvement will be considered a weakness. Think of improvements in terms of more time to coach them and respond quicker to them on their needs.

Question: As a manager, how do you make the work both fun and interesting for your employees?

Interpretation: This question seeks to gather information on how you think you make work enjoyable for your employees. What methods do you use?

Consider This: Always respond that keeping it light with a sense of humor and making yourself accessible to them 24/7 take the pressure off them.

Question: Tell me how some specific event in your past influenced your approach to relating to people.

Interpretation: In asking this question, the interviewer is looking for whether your relationship with people is more task-focused or people-focused. In other words, is your approach geared more toward interpersonal warmth and sensitivity, as opposed to reaching goals? Like many other questions, your answer to this question is a gauge of how well you'd blend with the company culture.

Question: In what kinds of social situations do you feel uncomfortable? Provide an example.

Interpretation: This question seeks to understand your level of comfort in dealing with social situations. If you are applying for a role in sales and you describe yourself as having social difficulties, be sure you explain the steps you have taken to improve your interpersonal effectiveness.

Consider This: A better approach if the position requires a lot of social interactions is to say this is the fun part of the position.

Question: Some people get to know strangers quickly, while others prefer to take their time letting people get to know them. Describe how you entered relationships when you were new on a job.

Interpretation: This question is all about how you will blend in with your new corporate setting. The interviewer is looking for evidence concerning interpersonal openness and willingness to enter into warm, supportive relationships.

Consider This: Being open, approachable, and responsive has always worked for you in developing relationships.

Question: If I was speaking with your superior and asked what major change was seen in you during the period he or she managed you, what would I be told?

Interpretation: This is one of those questions that asks you to see yourself as others see you. The typical answer involves giving an example of a weakness that was brought to your attention and how you have continued to work on resolving it.

Intraception

Intraception is the ability to interpret spoken and unspoken communications to develop accurate perceptions and understanding of others' needs, values, and opinions. The intraceptive candidate is a humanist capable of developing role-taking skills, as opposed to having a skeptical attitude. The intraceptive candidate is sensitive to and aware of political factors and the social environment, which is thought to be an important factor in the quality of moral decision making.

Question: How skillful do you think you are in sizing up people? Give an example.

Interpretation: This question seeks to determine if you have a well thought out approach for understanding people or whether you have a certain naiveté about individual differences. Needless to say, but let me say it anyway, naiveté is not what companies are looking for these days.

Consider This: Sizing up people is a learned process based on experience and you have that experience.

Question: Based on everything we have discussed so far about this position, if you were to be selected for the job, where are you likely to make your first mistake?

Interpretation: This question seeks to assess your level of understanding of the new position, which is a reflection of whether you did your homework, and your perceived area of weakness.

Consider This: Not understanding all the linkages internally to your actions.

Question: What are the critical factors you look for in evaluating the performance of a new employee? Give a specific example of when you used these factors.

Interpretation: This question seeks to determine whether you are aware of the fact that employees ought to be evaluated on the basis of behavior and performance, rather than on character

139

traits or personality.

Consider This: Results, goal attainment, interpersonal skills, and team fit.

Question: How important do you think money, responsibility, stimulating work, and recognition are to motivation? Can you give an example of these different forces at work?

Interpretation: This question provides the opportunity for you to demonstrate an awareness that different motivators work for different people. You need to explain, briefly and concisely, how different motivators work for various sorts of people.

Consider This: All are important but money normally is last because the enjoyment on the job is the key; achieving that, the money is never an issue.

Question: What has been the most political work situation you have experienced? Explain how you dealt with it.

Interpretation: This question requires you to reflect on the past and speak in non-negative terms as you describe whether you became actively involved in the organization's politics, withdrew from the situation, or took an aggressive stance.

Question: Do you find yourself to be the type of individual who is generally trusting of most people, or do you prefer to reserve the judgment until you get to know them well? Give an example that illustrates your tendency.

Interpretation: This question seeks to determine the extent to which you are naive or unaware concerning different motivations and abilities of others.

Question: Many people have the ability to step into another person's shoes. When has this skill been required of you?

Interpretation: This question seeks to assess whether you are able to empathize and give a specific, concise example of this trait. Are you able to appreciate someone else's emotions and understand how that person was feeling, or did you simply recognize them and understand them from a logical, detached perspective?

Question: When selecting a new employee, what is the most important trait you look for, and how do you determine if a candidate has that trait?

Interpretation: This question demands you make a decision on what you believe is the most important indicator of success and then make a judgment as to the presence or absence of that trait.

Consider This: The answer is high energy.

Introspection

Introspection is the ability to accurately examine your own thoughts and feelings and thereby understand your own strengths and limitations.

Question: How do you think your subordinates perceive you?

Interpretation: This question asks you to view yourself as others do. What management style do you think others think you use? Like many other questions, your answer to this one is a gauge of how well you will fit in the corporate culture.

Consider This: You answer is very fair and open to a discussion about any issue.

Question: How would you describe your own personality?

Interpretation: The interviewer, in asking this kind of question, is hoping to hear you mention two or three traits that demonstrate your balance and humanity. You need not be perfect, but you need to demonstrate some understanding of the need to improve in certain areas.

Question: What development areas would you have to focus on if you assumed this position?

Interpretation: This question expands upon the previous one. Do you recognize and understand the needs and skills required for the position? Do you have those needs and skills?

Consider This: Learning the organization, its people and roles that I will interact with to accomplish my objectives.

Question: What is your reputation in your current or most recent company?

Interpretation: This question tests your honesty, your self-awareness, and your understanding of how others perceive you. Does your reputation match your professed management style?

Consider This: You are proud of your reputation and your references will bear this out. I get things done on schedule, etc.

Question: Give me an example of what you would change or improve upon if you had the time and resources to work on a self-improvement program.

Interpretation: This question is a side-step approach to determine whether you have a self-improvement program in place.

Consider This: More education in regards to a technical area that you currently have an interest in and see a need for in the future.

Question: What are you looking for in your next job?

Interpretation: This question seeks to gauge whether there is a match, a near-match, or a complete mismatch between your desires and the reality of the job for which you are interviewing. The further apart your desires from the ability of the company to provide them in the job for which you are interviewing, the smaller the long-term relationship together. Companies don't enjoy wasting time and money filling the same position multiple times in short order.

Consider This: Challenge and growth opportunities and a team environment.

Question: With hindsight, how could you have improved your career progression?

Interpretation: This question seeks to understand whether

you are aware of your mistakes and weaknesses—in other words, whether you admit to having flaws—and whether and how you have worked to overcome them.

Consider This: Should have decided to move into the cutting edge technology when it hit the market, instead of remaining with the company an extra period of time.

Question: What are the reasons for your success in this profession?

Interpretation: This question seeks to determine whether you understand why you are successful. If you are in sales, what makes you better than another salesperson? How are your skills better or different?

Consider This: Your personal drive to succeed and eagerness to stay in the forefront of industry changes.

Question: In this position with ----, how would you want to be held accountable?

Interpretation: This question seeks to understand how you want to be managed. Your prospective manager is not likely to modify his or her style to accommodate you, so this information is a gauge of how well you will blend in and fit.

Consider This: I enjoy being told to take the objective; I clarify the parameters and accomplish my objective.

Leadership

Leadership is the ability to command through authority or influence. Do you demonstrate an ability to influence constructive action in others toward meeting objectives? Do you influence constructive actions in others over whom you have no direct control or position power? While leadership's skills can be taught, they can't necessarily be learned. The best leaders are natural-born leaders.

Question: How would your employees describe your leadership style?

Interpretation: This question seeks to understand how your staff perceives you. Your response should be balanced with both positives and negatives.

Consider This: Very open and approachable but firm on achieving stated objectives.

Question: What type of feedback, both positive and negative, have you received about your management style?

Interpretation: This question is a circle-back or follow-up to previous questions about your management style. The interviewer will be listening carefully for your negative comments and to see whether this answer matches up with your answers to previous questions on leadership.

Consider This: I will always give an employee a second chance to improve but never a third chance.

Question: Briefly review your leadership experience. Give examples that show what your leadership style is like.

Interpretation: This question seeks to determine whether you use an autocratic or persuasive leadership style and whether you are able to influence and be influenced without the use of power, status, or position. The quality of your past leadership accomplishments is a window to the future. Your answer to this question is also a gauge of whether and how well you will fit in with the corporate culture.

Question: Describe your best employees. What makes them good at what they do? How much influence have you had on them?

Interpretation: This question seeks to determine whether you implemented or supported development plans for your employees. If your current or previous employer did not support these types of initiatives and you implemented them yourself, this speaks highly of your management style. Don't sell yourself short.

Consider This: They all are high-energy people who do not take themselves seriously but take their work seriously. I have worked with them to always keep a positive outlook and with every setback, to find at least two positive outcomes.

Question: Did you learn anything about leadership from your parents? When and how have you applied their lessons?

Interpretation: This question seeks to understand whether your current style mimics your parental upbringing. Did you experience and do you now implement positive or negative attitudes in your leadership?

Question: Have you ever had to take over a leadership role unexpectedly? How did it work out?

Interpretation: By asking this question, the interviewer seeks to understand whether and how/how well you met the challenge. Did you adopt the predecessor's management style? Was the outcome successful?

Consider This: You want to have been asked to take over responsibility and overachieve in the role.

Question: What qualities do you look for in superiors?

Interpretation: Most candidates look for the same qualities in their managers that they see in themselves. By shining the light upward, the light is reflected back down to the candidate himself or herself.

Consider This: A leader with skills and experience one can learn from, as well as someone to model in one's self-development.

Question: How do you judge whether you are being successful managing your subordinates?

Interpretation: Your response to this question is meant to provide some insight into how you manage employees. It also serves as a gauge for whether and how well you will blend in with the corporate culture.

Consider This: The best example is when everyone wants to recruit away your employees because of your reputation for developing talent.

145

Larry Dillon

Question: When I contact your current or most recent superior, what is he or she going to tell me caused our meeting today?

Interpretation: Your answer to this question may offer the interviewer a glimpse of why you are in the market. Normally, the real reason is below the surface.

Consider This: The opportunity to grow and expand my skills. I am underemployed and have nowhere to go in the organization.

Question: What is your philosophy of management?

Interpretation: This question seeks to determine whether your stated philosophy is compatible with the current management philosophy of the position and the company. Don't expect things to change just for you. If you did your homework, you should know what the management philosophy is for this role and the company.

Motivation

Motivation is the quality of being inspired or impelled and the ability to inspire or impel others to carry out specific courses of action. Do you demonstrate motivation? Can you motivate others? Is this evident in your answers, your background, and your presence?

Question: Who is the most motivating individual you know? What characteristics do you have that are similar?

Interpretation: This question seeks to determine your definition of the characteristics associated with motivational individuals. Does your behavioral example show strength in motivation of others?

Question: What are some things that motivate you? How have you used these motivators with others?

Interpretation: This question seeks to identify your level of self-awareness of what you consider motivating and rewarding. The interviewer is listening to hear if you use these same motivations or rewards to encourage others. If not, why not?

Question: What things created excitement and cohesion in your current or most recent work group?

Interpretation: This question is meant to determine whether you can list specifics about work group togetherness and motivation. If you can recognize these characteristics, can you create them?

Question: Are you good at figuring out what will motivate someone else? When were you able to do this?

Interpretation: Good managers can motivate even the most unmotivated of workers. This question seeks to determine whether you appreciate individual differences in motivation and can apply that understanding.

Consider This: Being able to motivate others is a key requirement in selecting a manager.

Question: Can you give me an example of when you came up with a clever way of motivating someone?

Interpretation: This question speaks to your ability to apply creativity to the problem of motivation. Companies value those who can motivate others, particularly when the going gets tough.

Organizational Ability

Organizational ability is the capacity to organize or schedule people or tasks, to develop action plans leading to specify goals, and to plan effectively. Do you have these skills?

Question: How did you organize your work in your last position? What happened to your plan when emergencies came up?

Interpretation: This question seeks to determine whether you are aware of the importance of having a specific time for planning and organization. Did you allot time to establish work procedures? Did the plan you developed effectively deal with emergencies?

Consider This: The interviewer is listening for a well developed written out plan.

Question: Describe how you determine your priorities on your current or most recent job.

Interpretation: This question focuses on whether you defined priorities in terms of well-established, long-range approaches. The alternative is to simply react, which is not considered an effective management style. Do you provide evidence for establishment of priorities on a daily basis?

Question: Describe how you schedule your time on an unusually hectic day. Give a specific example.

Interpretation: This question requires you to consider specific elements in work scheduling. Did you control the environment or did the environment control you? Companies look for individuals who can apply control in the midst of chaos.

Question: What experiences have you had with budgetary decisions? What conclusions have you reached about how they ought to be done?

Interpretation: This two-part question gauges both your awareness of the negotiation process typically involved in developing budgets and whether you know that budgets are designed to reach objectives, rather than to simply expand functions.

Question: How far ahead do you plan? Can you tell me about a time when planning ahead (or not planning ahead) benefited you (or hurt you)?

Interpretation: This question addresses your ability to plan. Do you appreciate the value of planning ahead and anticipating problems? Do your long-range plans have sufficient flexibility to allow for unanticipated events? How specific are your plans? Are they realistic?

Consider This: This is the opportunity to really go into your experience in planning. Watch the interviewer for how much detail is needed, and ask if further detail is needed when concluding.

Question: Tell me about the workload in your current or most recent position. How do you divide your time among your major areas of responsibility?

Interpretation: This question is meant to analyze your time utilization and management skills and your attitude toward presumably heavy workloads. If this is a company where everyone stays until 8:00 p.m. every evening, your departure at 5:00 p.m. on the dot would be noticed.

Question: Tell me about a job or project for which you had to gather information from many different sources and then create something with the information.

Interpretation: The interviewer who asks this question is listening for the depth and quality of the information required for the job or project and its use in creating something with the information. The challenge is to be concise and specific, while tying together the skills of information gathering and product creation with the needs of the job for which you are interviewing.

Planning

The importance of planning is twofold and is gauged on your experience level and your ability to integrate analysis, organization, and planning into a process.

Question: Do you consider yourself to have been a good planner in your management roles thus far? Cite an example of what you consider good planning.

Interpretation: This is a double-edged question. Do you believe you are a good planner? What makes you believe this about yourself? The second part of the question is expected to yield some insight into what the candidate believes is good planning. If you have done your homework, you should know what kind of planning this company prefers to employ.

Question: What would you say has been your greatest hindrance in planning?

Interpretation: This question requires honesty about your acknowledged weaknesses and your self-awareness of what you should have done differently. Is your example of a greatest hindrance significant? Was it within your control to manage or eliminate it?

Consider This: In planning there is a need to quit revising a plan and take action.

Question: In order for me to understand how you think and plan, tell me how you plan your week in as much detail as possible.

Interpretation: This question provides the opportunity to describe your complete, organized plan. Demonstrate your natural ability to plan and organize your personal and professional life. If planning is a natural part of your personality, let it shine.

Policies and Procedures

Policies and procedures are the skeleton of an organization. Without them, there is chaos, inconsistency, randomness, unpredictability, and uncertainty. With them, there can be predictability, consistency, and constriction. Policies and procedures are subject to change, but it is not up to you to initiate changes to policies or procedures during the interview.

Question: Have you ever worked in a situation where there were continual changes in company operating policies and procedures? How did you react to the changes?

Interpretation: This question seeks to understand how you incorporate corporate changes into your own operating system. To what extent did you conform to the changes? Did you conform willingly or grudgingly?

Consider This: The answer to this question always is a willingness to adjust to changes.

Question: Can you describe a situation in which a company's policies and procedures have been unfair to you? How did you cope with the problem?

Interpretation: This is a tricky question to assess whether you feel embittered or resentful concerning policy application. Demonstrate your determination and motivation to conform to policy, even if you are in disagreement with it.

Consider This: Even if you feel you were treated unfairly, don't mention it; avoid any negatives that don't support your candidacy.

Question: Describe a situation in which you had to support the directives of higher management, even when you personally disagreed with them.

Interpretation: This question is your opportunity to demonstrate your ability to set aside your personal feelings in response to instruction from higher management. Do you look at higher management as "Them," those who make mistakes in leadership and decision making, while preferring to side with the attitudes and opinions of subordinates?

Consider This: Always focus on being a team player; management is paid to make the decisions.

Question: What types of policies have you found to be personally distasteful? Did you conform? Why or why not?

Interpretation: This question seeks to determine the extent to which you understand the role of policy in an organization. A history of failure to conform to policy is a red flag that the interviewer will not ignore.

Consider This: The best answer is you have not encountered this in your role.

Question: Have you ever been tempted to break policy for a special situation? If so, explain.

Interpretation: As a rule, companies don't like to hire rogues. This question is meant to assess whether you felt free to break policy for someone else and whether, if you broke policy, you first obtained permission to modify policy for a special situation.

Question: Have you ever had to deal with a subordinate who broke policy? How did you handle it?

Interpretation: This question assesses whether you are aware of the need to administer policy consistently to all individuals. The new hire who allows one person to break policy while enforcing the policy on others is probably not going to last long at the company.

Consider This: Answer that you took corrective action upon finding out about the problem.

Scope and Functional Influence

Scope and functional influence are indicators of the range or extent of organizational influence you have within the organization. The greater and broader your influence, the more likely you are to achieve the results you (and the organization) desire.

Question: Would you describe yourself as a futurist in the ---- industry? If so, how would you demonstrate your knowledge?

Interpretation: This question is meant to determine whether you conduct the kind of continuous research that enables you to stay current and will, in turn, allow the company to get ahead. What resources do you use and why do you use these particular ones instead of others?

Question: What would you say to someone who questions your depth of knowledge due to your one-company focus in technology?

Interpretation: This is a tricky question. . . .While you may be tempted to defend having worked for or promoted one company's technology, you must temper that impulse by weaving in information about your depth of personal research and study.

Consider This: If you have been backing a clear winner, there was no reason to switch to a loser, but you confirmed your decision by maintaining awareness of alternative technologies and companies.

Question: What words would you use to describe yourself? Why?

Interpretation: Most candidates describe themselves in flattering ways. This is not what the question is about. The interviewer wants to hear you speak about teamwork, commitment, and accomplishments. Mentioning creativity, technical awareness, and political sensitivity can't hurt either.

Question: With all the rapid changes that are currently underway in this industry, where would you place yourself on the technology curve? Why?

Interpretation: This is a tricky question. . . . You must find the middle ground so that you don't sound cocky but have a strong knowledge base.

Consider This: Give examples of how you maintain and expand your knowledge of technology to stay current.

Question: Thus far in your career, how many functional areas have you worked in? What was the scope of your responsibilities?

Interpretation: In these lean and mean times, employees and managers are often asked to wear many hats. Your answer to this question should demonstrate both breadth and depth of experience.

Consider This: This is the opportunity to expand on your experience beyond the role you are interviewing for at the moment. You may be considered for a completely different position.

Question: Describe how your job relates to the overall goals of the company.

Interpretation: This question is a way to demonstrate your knowledge of the company's goals. While you might not know all the goals of the company with which you are interviewing, you should at least know the goals of the company for which you work now or most recently worked. If you don't know the goals of your own organization, chances are you are not a true player in the organization.

Question: What standards does the organization use to evaluate your performance?

Interpretation: This is not a question about performance evaluations. Actually, this question seeks to understand whether you have a clear understanding of your strengths and limitations and how they are assessed and valued by the organization.

Question: What would you do during the first thirty days in this position?

Interpretation: Your answer to this question is a true signal of your personality. If you are conservative, you will likely opt to get to know the players in the organization. If you are aggressive, you will seek to initiate change before becoming aware of the possible interactions that support the current situation and the ramifications of making a rapid change. Unless you are under the impression an aggressive stance is desired, giving clues of an aggressive approach may be a red flag.

Shrewdness

Shrewdness is the quality of having a clever, discerning awareness of individuals and situations. Do you demonstrate a discerning awareness? Are you able to utilize acuteness in perception to gather and interpret information about the organizational climate and key individuals? Can you see around corners and through obstacles?

Question: Describe a time you were able to reverse a negative situation at work.

Interpretation: This question is actually twofold. First, you must prove your ability to recognize a negative situation and demonstrate skill in sizing up what makes the situation negative. Then you must execute the reversal in the situation's course to show real benefits to the organization.

Question: For what have you been most frequently criticized, and by whom?

Interpretation: The odds of getting a straightforward answer from a salesperson are slim; nevertheless, the question doubles as a way of testing the traits of quick thinking and poise that are necessary in sales. Even if your words communicate you have never received criticism for anything you've ever done, your body language and tone may yield some secret truths.

Consider This: You have been in a way criticized for always "being on."

Question: Describe a time when you proved to be more tenacious than your peers.

Interpretation: This is a tricky question that, in part, gives insight into how you view competition. When you speak about competition, do you think your peers are within the company or outside the company? Do you compete differently against one or the other?

Question: Many times being effective in a job means reading the system or figuring out what must be done to institute a change. Describe a time when you read the system. What were the results?

Interpretation: This question is meant to determine whether you understand how to read the system by taking advantage of the political forces in the organization. Your answer should speak to the interrelatedness of the various parts of the system. Your explanation of how you figured out how to effect change should show ingenuity and insight, rather than mere cleverness.

Question: Whom do you know who has been very effective in getting things done in a complicated working environment? What did they do? How are they like (or unlike) you?

Interpretation: This question is intended to show whether you recognize and can adapt the strategic methods and shrewdness of someone else. Be sure your answer identifies plausible strategies for effective change in a complicated environment. You don't need to have superhuman abilities to be shrewd; it's a personal skill you can cultivate if you are savvy, alert, and determined. Your example should make a clear connection between the other individual's personal skills and your own and show definite parallels.

Question: Politics at work is generally seen as being negative, but it is also clear that sometimes it is necessary to be careful about what you say and do. When have you found it necessary to be careful?

Interpretation: This question is tricky. Be careful to not speak negatively while demonstrating your appreciation for the possible ramifications of imprudent actions. Show you can identify and operate in a state of balance when those around you are tipping one way or the other.

Question: Different people have different hot buttons. When have you been successful in discovering what it really took to be successful in selling higher management (a coworker, or subordinate) on a change?

Interpretation: If you are in sales, this skill is critical. Even if you are not officially in sales, you will still need the ability to sell your ideas. This question is meant to determine whether you can show your ability to read others and employ good sense in terms of knowing when and how to seize an opportunity.

Question: Sometimes, it is important to be able to read hidden meanings in work communications. Describe a time when you were able to decipher a hidden meaning in a work-related communication.

Interpretation: This question is meant to determine whether you can see below the surface or read between the lines. This is not the time to appear naive.

Question: How do you think your job will differ twenty years from now as a result of technology?

Interpretation: This question is meant to test your ability to envision change in the distant future. If technology excites you, show your excitement. Don't jump on the couch, but be enthusiastic. Recognize that technology may marginalize people and, in order to sell that technology, those people would have to be brought into the fold.

Question: Do you know of any cases where someone has felt threatened by the introduction of new technology? What happened? What should have happened?

Interpretation: This question is intended to test your awareness of the impact technology can have on some people and allow you to prove you are empathetic. Your answer should show you are aware of methods, such as techniques to introduce technology, encourage participation, and promote involvement that improve the commitment to change and acceptance.

Question: What are some of the reasons that would cause you to turn down this position if it were offered to you?

Interpretation: This question is meant to determine whether your expectations of this position are realistic. Are your salary requirements in line with those being offered? Are your vacation expectations in keeping with company policy? The bigger the gap between your expectations and what the company is prepared to offer, the less likely you are to receive an invitation to join the club.

Consider This: This is a loaded question; the best answer is to say after your research on the company you are confident in the management and direction of the company and hope to play a role in its future success.

Strategic

A strategic individual has the ability to design and execute a planned effect. Do you demonstrate the ability to devise and employ plans or strategies toward a goal?

Question: Do you see yourself as a strategic thinker? If so, give an example to prove your point.

Interpretation: This is a straightforward question. Most candidates believe themselves to be strategic thinkers. The example you give must shed some light on your ability to think in strategic terms.

Consider This: Use an example of what you consider your

best strategic thinking and watch the eyebrows of the interviewer: up indicates surprise, maybe impressed, eyebrows down indicates disappointment.

Question: What important trends do you see coming in this industry?

Interpretation: This question offers the golden opportunity to prove your knowledge of the industry's trends and latest technologies and demonstrate your vision of what's next on the horizon. Do you have a "big picture" outlook? Trust that the interviewer, even if he is not particularly technically savvy, knows what's no longer current because he's done his homework. Prove you did yours too.

Question: If given this opportunity, how would you go about setting up a strategic plan for a worldwide marketing effort?

Interpretation: Even if you aren't directly responsible for marketing in the role for which you are interviewing, you might be called upon to contribute to the campaign in some capacity. This question is intended to determine whether you can devise the guidelines and approaches to developing a strategic plan.

Consider This: In any major management role this question may be asked and you should have a response prepared.

Task Management

Task management is the ability to establish and carry out specific courses of action for yourself and/or others. Task management and task completion demand a willingness to commit to long hours of work and personal sacrifice in order to reach goals. Do you have task management skills?

Question: Tell me your experience, in your current or most recent job, of "changing horses in midstream" (meaning frequent changes).

Interpretation: This question is intended to determine whether you can provide a specific example of the ability to juggle several tasks at once. Flexible work habits and the ability to handle multiple tasks in response to a rapidly changing environment are important in today's uncertain corporate world.

Question: Have you found it necessary to perform jobs that do not match well with your interests and abilities? Be specific.

Interpretation: This question seeks to determine the extent to which you were able to flexibly alter or set aside your personal desires and interests in order to get a job done. If you were able to do a job well even if it was distasteful, you should say so.

Consider This: The answer has to be that you can adjust to any situation if required and make a success out of it.

Question: When have you found it necessary to take work home?

Interpretation: This is, to a certain extent, a circle-back or follow-up question to commitment and time management. It seeks to validate those previously provided answers and probes the extent to which you organize and plan work so that you can do a good job in a reasonable amount of time and thereby avoid bringing your work home with you. If you regularly bring work home and your demeanor or message is one indicating insufficient commitment to work long hours, you may not succeed in this interview or the job for which you are being considered.

Question: Have you ever had to work with subordinates or peers who differed substantially in their abilities, attitudes, and personality characteristics? If so, how did you react to this situation?

Interpretation: This question is a circle-back or follow-up to questions regarding flexibility, versatility, and management style. It seeks to validate those previous answers and gather insight into whether you took sides in personality conflicts, the extent to which you got the job done in spite of significant interpersonal differences, and whether you assumed a leadership role to get the job done.

Question: Describe a situation in which you were expected to work with an individual whom you personally disliked.

Interpretation: This questions points directly to your level

159

of commitment. If you are committed to doing your job well and getting it done, you will do so despite your dislike of a particular coworker. The interviewer will use your answer to evaluate whether your level of results orientation is strong enough to overcome personal dislikes.

Question: Have you ever held a job in which you had the freedom to write your own job description? If so, how did you structure your work?

Interpretation: This question seeks to uncover information about your ability to flexibly define tasks and responsibilities in order to ensure the job gets done and done well.

Question: Many times pressure is exerted on an individual at work when the home/family environment changes. What have been your experiences in this area, and what did you do to adjust to the situation?

Interpretation: The interviewer who asks this question is trying to identify the extent to which home pressures might have lessened your ability to perform at work. Were you committed to maintaining your high level of performance at work and how did you accomplish this objective?

Team Building

Team building involves the ability to work with people in such a manner as to build high morale and group commitments to goals and objectives. Team builders need not be managers or leaders, but they do tend to be effective in these roles.

Question: As a manager, what would you be looking for when hiring people?

Interpretation: This is yet another circle-back or follow-up question that is linked to your management style and your ability to read people. Do you, as a manager, probe for whether their chemistry fits with the team, as well as their skills, initiative, and adaptability? If their skills, initiative, and adaptability are good but the chemistry with the rest of the team is wrong, the results will almost always be predictably bad.

Question: Tell me about a time when you managed employees who were jointly resistant to management.

Interpretation: This question is meant to determine whether you, as a manager, are aware of the forces that may cause employees as a group to resent and resist the directives of management. Did you side with the employees or with management? Was your position realistic and what was the outcome?

Consider This: This a real test of your management abilities. In answering the question you will need to explain why the employees were resistant and how you overcame it.

Question: In your present job, tell me about a time when you had difficulty getting others to establish a common approach to a problem.

Interpretation: This is another circle-back or follow-up question closely tied to your management style. It is intended to determine whether you planned and adhered to a firm strategy for team building, whether you adapted an existing approach, or simply used a "hip pocket" approach.

Question: Describe how you have coordinated the work of subordinates who disliked one another.

Interpretation: This question points to your willingness and ability to serve as a mediator to help establish common objectives for differing personalities. In the worst case, did you serve as a manager and discipline one or the other of them?

Question: Describe an experience in your background where you saw the working environment or management style weaken the attitude of teamwork and the overall resulting product. What did you do?

Interpretation: If you have encountered this situation, be careful to not speak about it in negative terms. Explain instead how the end product was adversely affected and what meaningful action you took or recommended to solve the problem.

Question: In your experience, has team sports taught you helpful skills that transfer to the workplace? Can you remember an important lesson you learned in sports that remains useful to you today?

Interpretation: This question seeks to determine, first, whether your background includes team sports, and second, whether you can articulate elements of team sports that are also common to group work activities.

Question: Tell me about an occasion when, in difficult circumstances, you pulled the team together.

Interpretation: Companies are always in search of a few good quarterbacks. This question is how the interviewer determines whether you might be one. He or she is listening for you to explain the approach you used and any unique techniques you used to pull your team together and move them forward.

Question: How did your manager get the best work out of you?

Interpretation: This is another circle-back or follow-up question related to management and motivation. It provides verification of previous answers and additional insight into what has motivated you in the past and might motivate you in the future.

Technical

Technical skills cover your technical knowledge, your understanding of technology, and your ability to utilize technical skills to accomplish the responsibilities of the position. You are assumed to be technically savvy if you are applying for jobs that require technical skills, but these questions are intended to weed out the posers from the true players.

Question: How would you describe your skill set?

Interpretation: Everyone has a defined set of skills. The interviewer is listening to determine which skills you believe you possess and the order of importance you place on them. Most people mention their strongest skill, or the one of which they are most proud or confident, first.

Consider This: Take the time to write out what you think your skill set is and refine it down to three or four major skills.

More than that number lessens the impact.

Question: If offered the opportunity to return for more education, what would you do with the opportunity?

Interpretation: The answer to this question may indicate an area of perceived weakness on your part or a lack of appreciation for the expense associated with training. If asked this question, clearly indicate whether you would be willing to pay for this training yourself, since this demonstrates a higher degree of commitment to learn from the experience.

Question: What was the most productive educational training you have received, and how did it help you in your current or most recent position?

Interpretation: This question seeks to determine your appreciation of the benefits of training based on productivity and your ability to be promoted.

Verbal Communications

Verbal communications involve the ability to use and comprehend words in a communication process. Verbal communications are essential to telephone conversations as well as face-to-face meetings. They are an integral part of business operations.

Question: It can be difficult to get a new idea accepted by others. When have you had to do this?

Interpretation: This question seeks to determine whether you use a well-defined strategy that emphasizes benefits to the listener. How well do you communicate in the interview?

Consider This: To answer this question you need a good example of trial and rejection before success.

Question: When have you felt that it was important to create graphs, charts, or tables for presentation?

Interpretation: Some people need to see information as

well as hear it. This question seeks to determine if you have had experience preparing and delivering both oral and visual presentations. Your answer should indicate your awareness that visually communicated information can enhance the impact of spoken words.

Question: Describe a problem person with whom you have had to interact. What did you say or do to reduce the level of conflict?

Interpretation: This question seeks to understand whether you could see the problem person's point of view. Did you encourage or discourage future communications? Was the method you used to handle this individual one that would be effective in the job under consideration? If you did your homework, you should have some idea of how this company treats the public.

Question: Describe the toughest communication situation you ever encountered. How did you handle it? What was the result?

Interpretation: Your answer will help the interviewer determine if you dealt with the situation effectively. He or she will assess whether the style of communication you used was well-suited to the demands of the task and role for which you are interviewing.

Question: What have been your experiences in making formal recommendations and oral reports to management?

Interpretation: This question seeks to determine if you have experience in communicating with authority figures. Does your example suggest that you can communicate well in the job under consideration?

Question: What has been your experience in making speeches to small groups . . . large groups?

Interpretation: This question is intended to ascertain whether you have experience in speech making and general oral communications. This skill is critical to roles that involve making presentations, whether to internal or external customers.

Question: Timing is very important to good communication. Describe a situation when your timing was good . . . bad.

Interpretation: This question seeks to assess your understanding of and appreciation for "timing," as well as your ability to manage time-sensitive communications. If you have done your homework, you should know how frequently this need will arise on the job for which you are interviewing.

Versatility

Versatility is the quality or state of being versatile, changeable, flexible, and multi-talented. Does this describe you?

Question: Who is the most demanding manager you have worked for? What was his or her management style?

Interpretation: This question seeks to prove or disprove your ability to work with authority figures. Did you acquiesce to authority and thus reduce commitment to do the job well? Was there evidence of successful adaptation that resulted in superior performance?

Question: When are you more formal or more informal as a manager? Describe a situation.

Interpretation: This question is intended to test whether you are aware of the utility of varying degrees of formality in different situations. Your answer should specifically demonstrate your ability to be versatile.

Question: Some people are said to have the ability to roll with the punches. Describe a situation where you demonstrated this type of skill in working with people. Be specific.

Interpretation: The interviewer is looking for you to show evidence of accommodation in lifestyle, habits, patterns, or preferences to meet the needs or demands of another person or situation. You will earn more points if you provide a concise and specific example of a significant business accommodation rather than a rambling example of some vague and personal accommodations.

Question: Many management theorists emphasize that it is important to have a plan through which we can win friends and influence people. What would you say has been your plan for achieving this goal in the past? Tell me about a specific time when your plan worked to your advantage.

Interpretation: This lengthy question seeks to determine if you had a specific approach to establishing friendships. For example, do you mention having a conversation about the other person's interests, establishing common interests, or avoiding talking about yourself? Your description of the approach should suggest adapting to others and being flexible.

Question: Is there anything that you feel is non-negotiable? If so, tell me about a time when that belief made people see you as inflexible or opinionated.

Interpretation: This question points to your ability to compromise. This can be perceived as a character flaw. If your examples of failure to compromise suggest difficulty in relating to others, the interviewer is likely to see a giant red flag waving over your head.

Consider This: Answer nothing is non-negotiable unless it is illegal or immoral.

Question: In order to be effective as a negotiator, it is important to not only be able to analyze your competition, but also to be able to compromise. Describe an experience in negotiating that reflects your ability to compromise.

Interpretation: This question seeks to determine whether you can assess and appreciate the other person's perspective and reach a compromise, rather than push your own single agenda.

Question: What is the most out-of-character thing you have done in your professional career?

Interpretation: Your answer to this question is a snapshot of the other side of your personality. Be careful what you reveal.

Consider This: Don't make yourself look foolish, or your credibility will be impacted.

Writing Communications

Writing communications involves the ability to write effectively and to extract information from written materials. Do you have writing communication skills? How effective are they?

Question: Have you ever been responsible for the creation of forms, checklists, work flow procedures, etc.? How did others evaluate your work?

Interpretation: This question seeks to evaluate your background and experience with creating and using written, structured communication formats.

Question: How do you feel about your ability to communicate in a written fashion? What kind of feedback have you received about your writing ability?

Interpretation: This question is designed to determine if you are comfortable with written forms of communication; some people aren't, and these people need writers and editors to help them. If you fall into this category, explain your efforts to overcome your reluctance with writing.

Question: In your current or most recent position, how often did you prepare written reports? How lengthy were these reports, on average?

Interpretation: For the candidate who isn't comfortable with writing communications, jobs involving extensive writing are pure torture. The interviewer needs to understand your level of experience in preparing written reports; your demeanor will indicate your level of comfort, regardless of what your mouth says.

Question: Describe the most elaborate (lengthy) report you have ever written. What aspects were the most difficult for you?

Interpretation: This question asks you to reflect on your history of writing lengthy reports. Chances are, if the topic was particularly important, the report was not merely a brief.

Position Factors

Controlling

Controlling involves taking charge, directing, managing, organizing, and supervising others. Some positions require an individual with skills at controlling. If the position for which you are interviewing requires these skills, you should ask yourself (because your interviewer will surely ask you) whether you have and can provide examples of these skills in your conversation.

Question: How do you challenge others to do their best? Give an example.

Interpretation: This question speaks to how you manage others and work with peers and leadership. Can you take control and bring out the best in others without engaging in confrontational challenges?

Question: What types of decisions do you feel are beyond the level of authority you have in your current (or most recent) job?

Interpretation: This question invites you to demonstrate awareness of decision-making responsibilities and limitations. Mention your past decision-making authority and show, based on your experience, that you are willing and able to take charge, if necessary, without usurping power that is not open for grabs.

Question: When have you had difficulty getting others to approach a problem as a unified team?

Interpretation: This question seeks to determine whether and how you planned a firm strategy for team building or simply let things transpire on their own. Demonstrate your ability to apply good leadership skills by being prepared to discuss your team-building strategies.

Question: What is your company's methodology in setting goals for its sales force? What input do you have and how successful have you been in exceeding your sales goals?

Interpretation: Even if the role for which you are interviewing does not directly involve setting sales goals, you will likely be called upon to contribute to the development or support of these goals. If you were not involved with goal setting directly, you should at least be able to speak to the topic of how your company set sales force goals; this knowledge proves your awareness of the interconnectedness of business operations. The key to the question is the methodology in goal setting; it should have a stretch element built into it.

Question: In your current job, do you trust your subordinates to get their job done? How do you know they get their jobs done? Describe a time when you were convinced of their worthiness (or unworthiness).

Interpretation: The trick to this question is to be direct. Do not prevaricate or give a vague, general response. You want to speak to specific feedback systems that provide information about the quality of subordinate performance.

Question: Describe how you manage your sales professionals. How much handholding do you do? Do you feel it necessary to be involved in a sale?

Interpretation: This question is another circle-back to questions targeting your management style. Again, even if you were not or will not be directly involved with sales, you were or likely will be tangentially involved. Speak to whether you manage from the top down or get involved with the details of each sale, or whether you merely stayed involved with the basics. Your homework should have told you which approach is preferred by the company with which you are interviewing.

Question: Describe a project for which you gathered multiple source information and then created a finished product.

Interpretation: Give a brief, concise, explanation that paints a balanced picture of your ability to get involved in directing, managing, and organizing information and others in an effective manner to produce a desired end result.

Persuasive

A persuasive person enjoys selling, changing the opinions of others, and convincing with arguments. A persuasive person negotiates with other people to achieve the desired objective.

Question: Describe a time when you sold an idea in difficult circumstances.

Interpretation: This question seeks to determine whether you have had experience applying your persuasion skills in difficult situations. Your answer should demonstrate your ability to effectively change the opinions of others. Be sure to touch on how you knew just the right balance between giving up too quickly and persisting too long.

Question: Explain techniques you use to overcome the objection of others.

Interpretation: Fully prepared salespeople enter into potentially sticky situations with a set of plans to win over others. If one argument fails, another is always at the ready. Does your answer to this question demonstrate your ability to formulate solid plans to win over others who pose objections?

Question: Give an example of how you identified a market requirement that was previously unnoticed. How did you present the opportunity to management?

Interpretation: This question investigates two skills: your ability to identify market requirements and your ability to persuade others of the importance of those previously unnoticed opportunities. First and foremost, the market requirement must be important and "significant" (revenue generating). Second, you must explain clearly and concisely how you were able to present it effectively to management.

Question: Describe your toughest sales presentation. What made it tough? What was the outcome?

Interpretation: This is a multi-part question. In answering

the first part, explain briefly what made the presentation difficult. In the second part, explain concisely how you overcame the obstacles.

Question: Describe a sales situation with a senior manager of a prospective company in which you were persuasive in getting the order. What technique did you use?

Interpretation: This question isn't as tricky as it might appear. You are expected to give an example of your best sales performance. The point is for you to stress that you implemented a verbal sell when the product would not sell itself.

Independent

Independent people have strong views on things and can be difficult to manage. They speak up, argue, and dislike structure. Being independent isn't necessarily a bad thing, but some companies value it more than others. If you are independent, do your homework to determine whether independence is a valued or shunned trait in your company of interest.

Question: What is the "gutsiest" thing you have ever said or done?

Interpretation: Most companies value a certain degree of independent assertiveness. Do you feel comfortable in this role? Explain concisely when you needed to be assertive and the results of your independent assertiveness.

Question: What is the most unpopular decision you have had to make?

Interpretation: Sometimes managers and leaders have to make unpopular decisions. This question seeks to determine whether you are particularly resilient or sensitive to situations involving criticism.

Question: Can you describe a situation in which you found it important to take a stand, even when the outcome was to your own disadvantage?

Interpretation: This question seeks to determine whether you are willing to assume a firm position and whether your position is an indication of high integrity or inflexibility. The situation about which you took your stand should be business-related and of sufficient importance to warrant your behavior.

Outgoing

Outgoing people are fun loving, humorous, sociable, vibrant, talkative, and jovial. These are positive traits, but must be balanced with professionalism and the seriousness required of the role for which you are interviewing.

Question: Describe a specific event in your past that influenced how you relate to people.

Interpretation: The interviewer evaluates your answer to this question according to your emphasis on the task aspects of a relationship rather than on the purely personal aspects of a relationship. Be sure to balance the need for interpersonal warmth and sensitivity with achieving the desired corporate objectives.

Question: How did you establish relationships when you were new on the job?

Interpretation: This question provides insight into your interpersonal openness and willingness to enter into warm, supportive relationships. You don't need to be best friends with everyone at work, but you need to demonstrate your ability to make friends and get along.

Affiliative

Affiliative people have many friends, enjoy being in groups, and like companionship. They are gatherers who attract and are welcoming of newcomers; for this reason, they are welcomed themselves.

Question: Most work situations require interaction with people we dislike. Describe how you handle this situation.

Interpretation: This question invites you to demonstrate your maturity and explain how you cope with individual differences. The interviewer gauges your answer according to your level of insight concerning your individual style and how you modified it to accommodate the disliked people. For example, did you reduce your gregariousness or resort to e-mail exchanges to avoid face-to-face encounters?

Question: As a manager, how do you make work both fun and interesting for your employees?

Interpretation: This is a circle-back question that challenges your ability to balance your employees' need for enjoyable work with getting the work done. Explain the methods you use and why you use them. For example, if you tried popularly recommended ones and found them lacking, explain why they didn't work.

Socially Confident

Socially confident people put other people at ease. They know what to say and are good with words, regardless of the situation. Social confidence is an essential skill.

Question: How do you handle talkative customers? How do you ensure that you are effectively communicating with them?

Interpretation: A certain skill is required to master the talkative customer and close the deal. Mention your ability to employ verbal repetition or your skill at quickly preparing written correspondence to emphasize points.

Question: What has been your experience dealing with customer pressure?

Interpretation: Even if you do not interact with external customers, you will likely have had and will continue to have experience interacting with internal customers, who may be even more demanding than the external ones. This question seeks to determine your depth and level of experience in coping with customer complaints and anger. Explain how you coped with and defused such pressures over a significant period of time.

Larry Dillon

If your coping mechanisms were particularly effective, explain why. If they weren't effective, explain what you learned from the experience and how you improved these skills.

Question: How do you react when you see colleagues disagreeing? Do you get involved or hold back?

Interpretation: This is, in part, a circle-back question. It speaks to your management style if the colleagues are your subordinates and to your social skills if the colleagues are your peers. Companies value mediation skills and, if you can serve as a mediator in interpersonal conflict, speak to this skill. If you can maintain a sense of calm when others are in disagreement, explain how you do it and the positive results you typically achieve.

Question: It's sometimes difficult to get new ideas accepted. When have you done this?

Interpretation: This question speaks to your skills of persuasion and your ability to read the other person to know what approaches are likely or not likely to work. Demonstrate your ability to apply a well-defined strategy that emphasizes benefits to the listener, based on your understanding of the listener and your having done your homework. The way you communicate during this interview is a perfect example of your skills of persuasion.

Question: What is your experience with making formal recommendations and oral reports to management?

Interpretation: This question delves into your experience communicating with authority figures. If you will have the ear of leadership in the new organization, you will have to have this skill. Be sure your examples suggest or, better yet, clearly state, your ability to communicate well in the job under consideration.

Question: Sometimes effectiveness in a job requires "reading the system" or determining how to institute a change. How do you do this?

Interpretation: This question seeks to determine whether you have the experience and skill to recognize and make best

174

use of the political forces in the organization. Demonstrate your awareness of the interrelationship of the parts of the system and how you came to that awareness. Be sure to communicate how your figuring out how to effect change showed ingenuity, insight, or cleverness, all of which are valued attributes.

Question: While political situations often arise in the workforce, it is also clear that discretion is necessary in certain circumstances. When have you encountered such a situation?

Interpretation: This question seeks to determine whether you appreciate the possible ramifications of imprudent actions. Demonstrate your understanding of the difference between office politics and general prudence.

Honesty

Honesty is demonstrated by behaving in a manner that is above reproach. The person in whom honesty is deep-seated is trusted, reliable, and a straight talker. It goes without saying, but I will say it anyway, that honesty is well valued. That said, there are times when a certain degree of prevarication (white lies) is required and must be administered judiciously. Knowing when to prevaricate can be a difficult lesson to learn.

Question: Recall for me a time when those around you were not being as honest or direct as they should have been. What did you do?

Interpretation: This question challenges you to describe how you tactfully redirected individuals to be forthcoming. The alternative—avoiding the situation by not speaking up and voicing your opinion—is probably not a good answer, although it may be warranted in certain situations.

Modesty

The modest person is reserved, avoids talking about himself or herself and his or her accomplishments, and is not status-conscious. By avoiding boastfulness, the modest person makes room for the accomplishments and successes of others.

Question: What could you bring to this position that someone else could not?

Interpretation: This question challenges your awareness of your skills and strengths relative to others' competencies. Now is a good time to mention concisely the parallels and connections between your experience and those required by the role.

Question: What is your success rate in achieving your goals?

Interpretation: Most candidates will attest to high achievement in accomplishing goals. The interviewer is listening for the facts that verify the statements.

Question: What do you consider to be your greatest achievement in your career for which peers or management recognized you?

Interpretation: This question seeks to understand whether you recognize how others perceive you, how you perceive your achievements, and how you perceive the impact/outcome of the achievement. It never hurts to speak in terms of revenue generated, costs avoided, schedules shortened, or increased number of customers satisfied by your performance.

Question: When have you had to "pull rank" over a peer in a work situation? What was the situation and how did you handle it?

Interpretation: This question challenges you to speak about a dicey situation without being boastful. You need to clearly and concisely explain why you felt the need to pull rank, whether and how you overcame the threat to your peer's ego or standing in the company, and the favorable or unfavorable business consequences of your actions. If you learned a lesson from the experience, convey it, but be sure to remain modest. It might have been something anyone else could have done, but it was you who did it.

Democratic

The democratic person encourages others to contribute. He or she consults with others, listens to what others have to say, and refers to others. Democratic individuals can be assertive without being abrasive because they recognize the presence of others.

Question: What do you consider assertive behavior in business situations?

Interpretation: The interviewer who asks this question is interested in your level of confidence and the degree of importance placed on listening to the other person.

Question: When are you formal or informal as a manager? Describe a situation where you have adapted your style.

Interpretation: This is a circle-back question related to your management style. Your answer should indicate your awareness of the utility of varying degrees of formality in differing situations and suggest your ability to be versatile.

Question: Describe how you coordinate the work of subordinates who dislike each other.

Interpretation: This is another circle-back question related to your management style and your ability to mediate. Your answer should indicate your ability to serve as mediator and establish common objectives for differing personalities.

Question: What are your experiences with scheduling the work of others? What problems arose? How did you handle them?

Interpretation: Yes, this is another circle-back question related to your management style. Good managers show concern for others along with concern for the task. Explain how your planning was done systematically, but that once a schedule has been made, you were able to incorporate small changes to accommodate people's needs.

Caring

Caring people are considerate to others and help those in need. They are sympathetic and tolerant. Be aware there is a definite line between caring and being a pushover. Caring managers are good; pushovers don't last long.

Question: Can you describe an experience in which you extended yourself to communicate with a problem person?

Interpretation: This question challenges your ability to concisely report your level of effectiveness in relating to difficult situations. You should neither resort to withdrawal or over-aggression in order to cope with the problem. This is a tricky question, because it requires you to describe the types of characters or the social dynamics that might also exist in the new position. Be sure to close your concise answer with a comment about how you have diligently applied strategies to overcome the challenges of working with people with whom you have had difficulty.

Question: When is the last time you stepped out of your lifestyle routine to accommodate the wishes of others? Be specific.

Interpretation: The challenge to this question is to present your explanation of a specific example in which you relinquished your personal preference to adapt to the needs of others without sounding wishy-washy or behaving like a doormat. While you might need to concede on occasion, it is possible this position requires a strong character that doesn't give in easily.

Question: Describe a situation where you felt that you were part of the problem. What did you do?

Interpretation: This question seeks to determine the measures you took to work toward a solution. The interviewer will use your answer to evaluate your ability to work with others' needs and provide a solution in a concise answer.

Question: What is the toughest decision you have made regarding a colleague? How did you go about it? What was the outcome?

Interpretation: This is a multi-part question. First, you must explain the situation that required you to make a difficult decision. Was it really a difficult situation? Did you approach the decision quickly or did you postpone your decision? What kind of values does your explanation emphasize and do you demonstrate consideration for individual values such as forgiveness and understanding or organization values such as policy and competence?

Question: What is your experience in dealing with the poor performance of subordinates?

Interpretation: Your answer must demonstrate your ability to make a distinction between private and public discussion of errors. Nobody likes to be called out in public: praise in public, reprimand in private. Your homework should tell you whether this company prefers to cut their losses quickly through termination or nurture a potentially valuable employee with career development to deal with the problem.

Question: Have you ever become involved in a problem faced by a coworker or subordinate?

Interpretation: This question seeks to determine whether you are more "other" oriented or self-oriented in responding to stress solutions. Do you seek self-solutions or are you able to direct attention toward helping others solve problems?

Question: Have you ever observed an employer de-motivating employees? What do you think was the underlying cause of the de-motivation?

Interpretation: This question seeks to determine whether you are aware that certain actions/statements, though well intended, may actually de-motivate employees. A good answer to this question is to describe a situation in which you did the opposite.

Practical

Practical people are considerate of others. They like repairing and fixing things, using their hands, and coming up with pragmatic solutions to problems.

Question: In your company, what are the policies concerning employee transfers? What problems occur?

Interpretation: When asked within a series of other "practical" questions, this question may seek to determine whether you are aware that transfers can mask a performance problem by passing individuals from department to department. It seeks to determine your awareness that rigidly enforced policies can work against the true goals of the organization.

Question: Have you ever dealt with a subordinate who broke policy?

Interpretation: This question seeks to determine your understanding of the corporate standard that policy must be consistently administered to all individuals but that compassion can be applied to ease the impact.

Data Rational

The data rational person likes to work with data and operate on facts. He or she enjoys assessing and measuring situations based on facts.

Question: Describe a situation in which you made a decision even though you did not have all the information.

Interpretation: This is a tricky question. No decision is made with all the facts. What is being evaluated is your ability to make decisions. Managers make decisions. Your answer should indicate your awareness of the importance of having all the facts before making a decision, even if it means deferring a decision for a brief time. There are times, however, when an immediate decision must be made even though all the facts are not available, and your answer should indicate how you concluded that a decision could not be deferred, what facts were missing, and what lessons you learned from having been in that situation.

Question: Growing companies can have a difficult time responding to the demands of potential customers. How do you determine to which potential customers you direct your attention?

Interpretation: This question seeks to determine whether you have a systematic approach to define which customers have highest priority. Your homework should have told you which clients, companies, or industries have most favored status.

Question: Occasionally, we face situations that cause us to think negatively about our abilities, regardless of what our assets may be. Describe your experiences in this type of situation and recount how you decided what to do.

Interpretation: This question seeks to determine whether you avoided making a decision at all in the face of self-doubt, the extent to which you were able to objectively evaluate the situation, or whether you overreacted and made the decision on a purely emotional and not rational basis.

Question: If you had the opportunity, what one business decision would you rethink? Would you do anything differently?

Interpretation: This is a circle-back question to the process you use to make decisions. If you used all the tools available when you first made the decision, there should be no need to revisit it.

Question: What is the biggest career decision you have made? How did you arrive at your decision?

Interpretation: This question seeks to determine whether you are analytical and thoughtful, or speedy and impulsive in coming to a decision.

Question: What steps have you taken in deciding to terminate an employee?

Interpretation: This question seeks to determine whether you collected information associated with performance before or

181

after you made the decision to terminate. Obviously, the correct answer is to indicate you gathered this information and then based your decision on the information. Under no circumstances would you have made such a decision based on personality or politics.

Question: What types of decisions or judgments do you make in your current position or did you make in your most recent position? How did you reach those decisions?

Interpretation: This question seeks to understand your level of responsibility and approach to decision making. Your answer should indicate you first appreciate the ramifications of the decision that needs to be made and then you gather the facts and assess them. You consider your various options and then you make a well informed and carefully thought out decision.

Artistic

Artistic people appreciate culture and are sensitive to visual arts and music. In business, artistic people can apply their vision to actuate innovative solutions.

Question: Do you feel that graphs, charts, and so on are essential or important for presentations?

Interpretation: Your homework about the company and position should give you a clue about how to answer this question. The question actually telegraphs the answer. Of course they're important! Your answer should describe your experience with creating oral and visual presentations. Mention how visually communicated information can enhance the impact of written and spoken words.

Question: How would you characterize your interest and reaction to your work surroundings—functional or aesthetic?

Interpretation: This question seeks to determine whether you are sensitive to how things appear aesthetically, which would shed light on your concern for your work output in general.

Question: Do you favor attending functions dealing with arts such as music and literature, or functions involving sports activities? Why?

Interpretation: Some positions require a level of social and cultural engagement. If the position under consideration requires you to participate in cultural activities, this question helps to determine both your comfort level in this type of setting and your preference for one type of social engagement over another.

Question: What are your favorite activities or means of entertainment outside of work?

Interpretation: This question seeks to gather information on whether you have an appreciation for the arts and to what extent you are involved in cultural activities.

Behavioral

The behavioral person analyzes thoughts and behavior. He or she is psychologically minded and likes to understand people.

Question: Describe any areas where you do/did not feel comfortable with your present or most recent manager.

Interpretation: This is a tricky question. You don't want to mention matters of personal or professional style, which might carry over to the next superior. Instead, consider addressing issues involving poor vertical communication or other areas about which you know, based on your experience, the company with which you are interviewing excels.

Question: Describe a relationship with a colleague in which you were unsure of his or her feelings. How did you handle it?

Interpretation: This question seeks to identify your level of skill in discovering another person's feelings while behaving in an interpersonally effective manner. This is a particularly important skill in positions involving sales.

Question: Describe one or two areas that you and your manager disagreed on.

Interpretation: This is a circle-back question to the one involving your comfort level with your current or most recent manager. If you and this manager were prone to disagreements, that behavior might carry over to the next superior.

Question: Have you ever been told that you were too pushy or too nice on the job? What did you do that prompted the comment?

Interpretation: This is a circle-back question to validate your interpersonal performance, how others perceive you, and your ability to utilize feedback to change your behavior.

Question: Do you think that everyone has the capacity to be creative? What experiences lead you to this conclusion?

Interpretation: This question seeks to determine whether you have a theory of creativity. Do you think creativity is a gift or is something that can be developed? In the position under consideration, will you expect creativity only from certain employees?

Question: What types of decisions or judgments do you make in your current position or did you make in your most recent position? How do you reach those decisions?

Interpretation: This is a circle-back question to your level of responsibility and approach to decision making. Remember, be concise in listing those areas or tasks for which you had responsibility.

Question: Have you ever worked with subordinates or peers who differed substantially in their abilities, attitudes, and personalities? If so, how did you react to this situation?

Interpretation: This question seeks to gather insight into whether you were able to remain impartial in personality conflicts and the extent to which you were able to get the job done in spite of significant interpersonal differences. Your answer should mention how you assumed a leadership role to get the job done.

Question: List five important guidelines you use in evaluating people. Why do you use these parameters?

Interpretation: Your answer to this question should prioritize task-related characteristics over interpersonal factors, but not disregard the interpersonal factors completely. After all, a group of top-performing individuals who cannot be made to get along with each other is not an effective group.

Question: What experience do you have in dealing with irate customers?

Interpretation: Your answer to this question allows the interviewer to evaluate your ability to effectively communicate in a conflict environment. Explain concisely the steps you have taken to defuse conflict, mitigate anger, and resolve issues through good listening and response skills.

Question: Describe a high morale team with which you worked. Who was responsible for creating the motivation? What did they do?

Interpretation: This question seeks to determine whether you are aware of various popular energizing/motivational techniques or whether you have developed your own techniques.

Question: When have you seen effective motivators fail? What did you learn?

Interpretation: Sometimes even the best motivators fail and there are lessons to be learned from those failures. Demonstrate your having learned the lesson by explaining how you use good judgment in selecting motivators.

Question: Thus far in your career, what have you learned about motivation and how have you applied these concepts?

Interpretation: This is a circle-back question to your management style. Your answer should reinforce your previous answer to this same question and demonstrate your understanding that individuals have different motivators. If you have developed any motivational techniques and applied them successfully, be sure to mention them.

Question: It is occasionally necessary to read the hidden meanings in work communications. When did you have to decipher a hidden meaning in a work-related communication?

Interpretation: The trick to this question is to be succinct in explaining when and how you demonstrated your ability to see beneath the surface or read between the lines.

Change Oriented

The change-oriented person enjoys doing new things, seeks variety, and prefers novelty to routine. He or she accepts and welcomes changes in work and personal life.

Question: What major obstacles have you overcome on your past jobs?

Interpretation: This question challenges you to evaluate your career and provide a concise answer demonstrating your awareness of obstacles and your ability to apply various specific approaches to solve problems.

Question: How necessary is it for you to be creative in your job?

Interpretation: When the job requires strict adherence to policies and procedures, high degrees of creativity are often not desirable. The best answer to this question is a statement regarding flexibility or your skill at incorporating creativity into everyday activities.

Question: Describe a situation where you demonstrated the ability to "roll with the punches."

Interpretation: Provide evidence of accommodation in lifestyle, habit patterns, or preferences to meet the needs or demands of another person or situation. The trick is to do so briefly, then ask if additional details are desired.

Question: Describe your experiences with reprioritization.

Interpretation: Business priorities change frequently. This question seeks to determine if you can multi-task. Your example should demonstrate flexible work habits in response to a rapidly changing environment.

Question: Can you tell me about a time when your carefully laid plans went afoul? How did you react? What happened?

Interpretation: This question seeks to determine whether you are a slave to your plans. Of course you're not! Your answer should clearly and concisely list your strategy for calmly reformulating your plans as the need arises.

Question: Describe a time you reversed a negative situation at work.

Interpretation: This question seeks to identify your skill in assessing a situation and turning around a bad one. Your answer should quantify the extent to which your turnaround solution provided real benefits to the organization, either in terms of time or money saved or revenue generated.

Question: Do you know someone who is very effective in getting results in a complicated working environment? What does she or he do? How do you do this?

Interpretation: There always seems to be one person who manages to get things done in the midst of chaos. Even if it's not you, you are expected to be able to learn something from that person. What plausible strategies for effective change in a complicated environment were you able to glean from that person? Your answer should not denigrate others or attribute credit to the effective person's luck or superhuman abilities. Ideally, your example should highlight your own personal skills in this area.

Question: Give me an example of a common practice in ----, which you feel is outdated but is widely utilized today. How do you deal with it?

Interpretation: The interviewer who asks this question typically fills in the blank with whatever industry the company is involved in or whatever department the position for which you are interviewing is located in. Your answer should indicate your respect for conventional methodologies that continue to work and your ability to incorporate pioneering new methods as needed.

Question: What is the relationship between maintaining effective job descriptions and the development of a sound teamwork atmosphere?

Interpretation: This is a circle-back question to your style of management and ability to promote teamwork. Teamwork is related to good job descriptions and the collective understanding of where each person's job begins and ends, but there is more to building a good team than just writing good job descriptions. Your answer should demonstrate this awareness.

Question: On reflection of situations in which achieving goals was difficult, what would have been a better way to establish, monitor, and accomplish business goals?

Interpretation: This question seeks information about your creativity, your ability to identify and resolve problems, as well as possible problems carrying out objectives in your current or most recent position.

Question: What important goals have you set and how successful were you in accomplishing them?

Interpretation: The trick to answering this question is to be concise and list the goals with which you were successful. Your goals should be business-related and realistic to both motivate and challenge.

Innovative

The innovative person generates ideas, shows ingenuity, and thinks up solutions. Innovative people are welcome in almost all business settings, except perhaps accounting, where creativity is frowned upon.

Question: Personnel policy may cause some problems while solving others. When have you seen this situation occur and how did you deal with it?

Interpretation: Companies have personnel policies for good reason, even if those reasons are not always apparent. Your answer should include a statement regarding your awareness of the need to apply personnel policies in the face of personnel problems while remaining sensitive to the problems themselves. Be prepared for a follow-up question about how you handle personnel problems for which no policy exists.

Question: When did you use your creative talents to solve a business-related problem?

Interpretation: This may be your best channel of creativity. . . . Make sure your answer involves a business-related problem and is reinforced by quantifiable details such as time saved, cost avoided, or revenue generated.

Question: With regard to marketing and sales, do others think you are a creative person? Describe the circumstances.

Interpretation: Most people believe themselves to be creative, but you are asked to prove it. Your example must support your claim of being creative.

Question: What task do you consider to be the biggest waste of time? How would you change it?

Interpretation: The most frequent response to this type of question is meetings. Your answer should describe, in brief, your method for creatively reducing the time wasted in meetings, group sessions, and the like.

Question: Some creative individuals require a stimulating work environment to facilitate their productivity, while other creative personalities are productive regardless of their immediate environment. What steps do you take to create a stimulating work environment?

Interpretation: This is a circle-back question to your management style. It seeks information on whether you understand the relationship between creative skills and the work environment and the extent to which you will modify or enhance the work environment in order to promote creativity.

Because the extent to which you can modify or enhance the work environment may exceed the scope of the position for which you are interviewing, your preference should correspond with the job under consideration.

Question: Describe a time when you reversed a negative situation at work.

Interpretation: Your answer to this question provides insight into your skill in assessing the situation and yielding real benefits to the organization, either in time or cost saved, revenue generated, or opportunities/clients salvaged.

Question: Do you consider yourself to be a good planner in your management roles? Cite an example of what you consider good planning.

Interpretation: This is a multi-part question. Obviously, everyone thinks they are good planners, but what makes you a better planner than someone else? Explain what makes for good planning and why you believe you are a good planner.

Question: What role does planning play in your activities?

Interpretation: All candidates respond positively to questions involving planning. The key to distinguishing yourself from other candidates is in your example of planning. It should be well thought out and demonstrate the ability to set and achieve goals.

Question: Have you worked in a situation in which there were constant surprises or unanticipated events coming to your attention? How did you deal with them?

Interpretation: Constant and repeated emergencies are a sign of poor organization. This question seeks to determine whether you are able to develop plans and strategies so that surprises will not recur in the future.

Question: How do you feel about the workload at your current (most recent) position? How did you divide your time among your major areas of responsibility?

Interpretation: Most companies nowadays expect their employees and management to be able to multi-task. There is no such thing as too much work if one is well organized and can prioritize. Your answer will provide the interviewer with insight into how you utilize time and your attitude toward workload.

Conscientious

The conscientious person sticks to deadlines, completes jobs, preserves routines, perseveres through obstacles, and fixes flawed schedules, processes, and products.

Question: Sometimes it is very important to adopt a "wait-and-see" attitude on the job. Give an example of when you were in this position. What did you do?

Interpretation: This question seeks to determine whether you exhibited appropriate behavior relative to the described situation. Be sure your answer explains why you deferred taking action, how long you waited until you took action, and what you learned by having waited instead of acting immediately.

Question: Give an example from your current job that demonstrates your persistence.

Interpretation: This question seeks two pieces of information: your definition of persistence and an example of when you thought it was appropriate to be persistent. Your answer should clearly demonstrate your awareness of the difference between being persistent and being a pest.

Question: What roles do you play in setting goals for a marketing and sales team? Which goals are the most difficult to achieve? When have you renegotiated a goal commitment?

Interpretation: This is a circle-back question to reinforce your understanding of your role in the organization and your ability to work with others. Even if you are not directly involved with marketing and sales, you will be expected to support their

191

initiatives to achieve the organization's goals. Your answer should indicate your ability to establish realistic, achievable goals and commit to them.

Relaxed

The relaxed person is calm, cool under pressure, and free from anxiety. He or she gets things done without entering panic mode.

Question: Give an example of stress in your current (or most recent) position. How have you learned to cope with stress?

Interpretation: This question does not ask whether you encountered stress but how you handled it. Your answer should be work-related and, if possible, similar to the type of stress you are likely to encounter in the position for which you are interviewing. If you are accustomed to working under pressure, be sure to say so.

Question: What do you do while waiting for the results of an important decision (e.g., career, medical, financial, personal)?

Interpretation: This question seeks to understand how you behave in potentially stressful situations over which you have no control or influence. If you are able to remain calm while awaiting any sort of potentially life-altering information, you should be able to transfer that coping mechanism to the work setting. Your answer might indicate some physical outlet, such as engaging in sports or gardening, some distraction, such as reading or chatting on the phone, or your willingness to seek spiritual or family support.

Question: Tell me about a time when you had problems or stresses that made it difficult for you to cope.

Interpretation: This question seeks to determine the extent to which you are able to manage stress in either your personal or professional life. If you have developed coping mechanisms that have worked for you in the past, you should be able to apply those same coping skills to your fulfillment of this role.

Question: What are your experiences with home/family issues creating work stress?

Interpretation: It is illegal for an interviewer to ask about your personal life, but this question skirts the issue by asking about how your personal life affects your performance at work. Your answer should indicate your ability to maintain your performance at work regardless of what might or might not be going on in your personal life.

Tough-minded

Tough-minded individuals are difficult to hurt or upset. They are unflappable and can brush off insults. They are unaffected by unfair remarks. Be aware there is a difference between being tough-minded (which can be a good thing) and being stubborn (which is rarely positive).

Question: Describe a situation where higher management challenged one of your decisions. How did you react?

Interpretation: This question seeks to understand how you react to criticism from those in authority. Your answer should demonstrate your ability to explain maturely, respectfully, and without emotion the rationale for your decision, rather than acquiescing to authority.

Question: Describe a situation in which your work was criticized. Did you feel the criticism was fair?

Interpretation: Criticism should always be professional, not personal. Even the harshest criticism can be cast in a positive light. When it is not, you may be challenged to remain calm and move beyond it. You must have thick skin. Your answer should indicate your ability to deal with and accept criticism in a positive manner.

Emotional Control

Individuals with emotional control are self-restrained. They maintain awareness and control of their emotions, keep their feelings to themselves, and avoid outbursts. They are unflappable and they are valued in business settings.

Question: Describe a time you postponed making a decision even though you felt frustrated in holding back.

Interpretation: This question seeks to assess your ability to postpone action in the face of frustration. We all get frustrated at times, but the best of us remain calm and think before taking actions that might be rash.

Question: What types of things make you angry? How do you react in these situations?

Interpretation: This question seeks to determine whether you have a quick temper. Even if you do, you should be able to control any hostile feelings so as to avoid social conflict. Nobody wants to hire or work with a ticking time bomb.

Critical

The person who thinks critically likes probing the facts. He or she is able to see the disadvantages and challenge the assumptions.

Question: Tell me about a job or position you should not have taken. How did you resolve the problem? How long did you remain in the job?

Interpretation: This is a tricky question. You don't want to sound as though you made a bad decision when, in fact, you did just that. Your answer should provide insight into the lessons you learned from that experience. Explain how you became aware of the bad fit and that, upon realizing the mistake, you left after giving the situation a reasonable period of time to right itself.

Question: Describe an experience in which you saw the working environment or management style weaken the teamwork attitude. What did you do?

Interpretation: This is a tricky question in that it asks you to critique someone else's management style when that might be the preferred style at the organization with which you are interviewing. The best approach to answering this question is to be certain to describe how the situation inhibited teamwork. If you or someone else took meaningful action, explain how that took place. If the idea or guidance related to the action was yours, be sure to say so!

Question: What has been your greatest hindrance in planning?

Interpretation: This is a two-part question. First, explain your definition of hindrance. Is it a small obstacle or a big brick wall? Next, explain why that hindrance is beyond your control and how you worked to resolve the hindrance. If you worked with others, be sure to explain how you garnered their support.

Active

Active people exude energy. They move quickly, keep busy, don't sit still, and overcome challenges through creative, carefully directed forward momentum.

Question: Describe a healthy staff meeting you have been in, as well as an unhealthy staff meeting.

Interpretation: Business-savvy individuals know staff meetings are time-wasters. Explain that group discussions and brief get-togethers tend to yield more enthusiastic participation and positive results.

Question: Describe a project that required you to deliver a high degree of energy over an extended period of time. What did you do to maintain your enthusiasm?

Interpretation: This question seeks to understand not whether you can generate self-motivation (it assumes you can) but how you maintain it and translate it into enthusiasm. Enthusiasm is contagious; even only one enthusiastic participant can turn a sluggish group into a band of go-getters. Deliver your answer with enthusiasm and increase your credibility.

Question: In what physical activities do you participate and how do you maintain your energy when engaging in those activities?

Interpretation: Part of the reason for asking this question might be related to the organization's interest in sports or their awareness of their customers' interest in sports. Many deals are sealed on the golf links or behind home plate. Individuals who engage in team sports are, by nature, team players, while those who observe sports may still appreciate and support the enthusiasm associated with sports. Your answer, whether it makes mention of tennis, golfing, or bowling, should be delivered with energy and vitality.

Question: How would you describe the energy you have as one point along a continuum; would it be marshaled intensively for specific projects or applied evenly across everything you do?

Interpretation: This question seeks to determine whether you have the same level of excitement for everything you do. It's not unusual to experience lulls or inactivity, but if only one thing excites you and that thing is sports—not work—then the interviewer might see a red flag waving over your head.

Competitive

The competitive individual plays to win. He or she is determined to beat others, regardless of the game.

Question: How important is it for you to win in a sales confrontation? How do you recover when you lose?

Interpretation: This question is transparent and so is the answer. The correct response might be that winning is always the objective. The way to recover is to not give up on the sale, but find a way to stay in the running.

Question: Has anyone ever described you as a "tiger" or go-getter? What were the circumstances?

Interpretation: This circle-back question seeks to re-assess whether you appreciate how others perceive you and whether you take pride in their perceptions of you. Assertiveness and aggressiveness are similar characteristics, but aggressiveness has decidedly negative connotations. Being proud of aggression will not be viewed favorably.

Question: Tell me your definition of "competitive" in a work environment.

Interpretation: While a certain degree of competition between colleagues might be healthy, the most productive type of competition in the office is between an individual and himself or herself. Your answer should indicate your preference for deriving satisfaction from attaining self-imposed goals and objectives.

Achieving

Achieving people are ambitious and set their sights high. They are career centered and results oriented.

Question: Describe an event that really challenged you. How did you meet that challenge? Was your approach different from others?

Interpretation: Achievers don't like second place. Their ambition drives them in everything they do. If you are an achiever, you should have little difficulty coming up with any number of examples to answer this question. Try for one related to business, perhaps demonstrating an achievement that bested a competitor.

Question: When I contact your past managers, what examples will they choose to demonstrate your ability to achieve your objectives?

Interpretation: This is, in part, a circle-back question to your awareness of how others perceive you and your performance. Your answer should indicate your ability to persevere in accomplishing objectives in the face of obstacles or discouragement.

Question: What do you regard as the most creative activity in which you have engaged? Did it bring you recognition, financial reward, or personal satisfaction?

Interpretation: While this appears to be a question related to your personal life, it's not really that at all. It seeks to determine whether you associate accomplishment with the creative act itself or with the results of the act. In terms of business, it's all about results.

Question: How long does it typically take you to close a sale from initial contact with the customer?

Interpretation: Your answer to this question telegraphs your approach to sales and whether it fits with that of the organization. The two most common approaches are to either move in quickly and aggressively for the close or wait until the prospect makes the decision. Most companies interested in generating revenue prefer the former approach.

Question: Have you ever taken over an existing territory? What was the volume when you started and when you left or after you'd managed it for a period of time?

Interpretation: Salespeople generate and close deals. Any market that has been left as it was found denotes a lack of skill, effort, and knowledge of market penetration and development techniques. Be sure, if you are in sales, you can speak to how you've increased sales for your territory or have a really, really good reason why not.

Question: What happens when you fail to meet a goal? How do you feel? Give me a specific example of such a time.

Interpretation: This question seeks to determine whether you set realistic goals and achieve them. You should be able to provide feedback on why you did not achieve your goals and it should include constructive conclusions. Your answer should demonstrate flexibility in setting goals so they can be adjusted relatively easily and quickly to meet the demands of the particular situation.

Question: Do you tend to set goals that are easily attained or ones that are too difficult to reach? Tell me about a goal you set that was too easy or too difficult. What did you learn from the experience?

Interpretation: While setting stretch goals is a way to challenge yourself, consistently failing to achieve them is not ideal. Your answer should demonstrate your ability to set reasonable goals. Any feedback you receive should be converted into action that allows you to recalibrate goals. Your answer should include details about the information you use to establish goals; it should *not* indicate you set goals using gut feelings.

Question: What is your current or most recent company's methodology in setting goals for its sales force? What input do you have and how successful have you been in exceeding your sales goals?

Interpretation: The key to this question is the methodology in goal setting. It should have a stretch element built into it so that the sales force is challenged to achieve it.

Decisive

Decisive people are quick to reach conclusions. They assess situations rapidly, sometimes hastily. Decisive people take risks.

Question: Describe the riskiest business decision you made. How did it work out?

Interpretation: This question seeks to determine if you are aware of risks involved in decision making. It assesses your willingness to make decisions in a risky environment or whether you prefer a more cautious approach.

Question: Cite an example of a decision you made without consulting a superior or supervisor. What is your level of authority?

Interpretation: Your response to this question provides insight into the level of decision making you are accustomed to making. If it is substantially lower than that of the role for which you are interviewing, be prepared to explain why you believe you can handle more responsibility than that given by your current or most recent employer.

Question: Describe a situation in which you made a rapid decision.

Interpretation: This question allows the interviewer to assess your behavior in answering the question, as well as the answer itself. Your answer should demonstrate your understanding of the pros and cons of speedy decision making.

Question: How does your current decision-making responsibility create risks for your employer? Are you acutely aware of the risks?

Interpretation: This question seeks to assess your awareness of the potential consequences of poor decision making. Your answer should indicate your involvement with maintaining balance sheets or tracking performance, particularly performance resulting from decisions you made, against projections.

Organizational Approach

These questions focus on how you approach the organization and this position.

Question: If you've done your homework, then you'll be able to relate some of your experiences in solving problems to those you'd likely encounter in this position.

Interpretation: This is where the rubber meets the road. This question challenges you to prove you are prepared for the interview and are actually capable of filling the position.

Relevant Accomplishments

These questions focus on your accomplishments and how they might be applicable to the organization and this position.

Question: In your recent position, what were two of your most significant accomplishments?

Interpretation: Your answer to this question should indicate that you had significant accomplishments (the best ones are quantifiable) and whether they are applicable to the organization at which you are interviewing.

Question: If you were to get this position, where do you think you would make your first mistake and what do you think it might be?

Interpretation: Your response to this question provides insight into an area you may perceive as a weakness.

Question: If I called your current or most recent manager, what would he or she tell me precipitated our meeting today?

Interpretation: Your answer to this question may offer a glimpse of why you are in the market and what motivates you. Be sure to cast yourself in a positive light.

Question: Give me an example of a business situation where you were effective as a negotiator. What did you do?

Interpretation: Your answer to this question probably reflects your most recent accomplishment.

Question: How are you apprised of your performance? Tell me about your last performance review.

Interpretation: Many managers do not receive written reviews. The purpose of the question is to determine whether a written review exists. If there *is* a written review, you can bet your interviewer will ask for it when he or she performs the reference checking. Be aware that some companies do not share this information about current or former employees and, if this is the case, you might want to mention it so that your interviewer doesn't walk away with the feeling he or she has been stonewalled because of a pending lawsuit.

Softball Questions

Prior Positions

These questions focus on your performance in past positions. The answers will likely be a predictor of your performance in this position too.

Question: What makes you unique in your position?

Interpretation: This is a defining question on how you view your own importance.

Question: Why do you suppose you were selected for your current (or most recent) position?

Interpretation: This question seeks to determine whether you can point to performance accomplishments. If you do point to performance accomplishments, be sure they are significant and business-related.

Question: In what ways did you exceed your manager's expectations?

Interpretation: Your answer should include specific accomplishments in achieving business objectives similar to those of the company with which you are interviewing.

Question: In your current (or most recent) position, what were the things you liked the most and the least?

Interpretation: If the same issues are present in the company or opportunity for which you are interviewing, you just ended the interview. Your homework should provide clues about the social and political scene at the company.

Question: Describe a position where you really had to concentrate on the details of the task or responsibility. What made it detailed?

Interpretation: In some aspects of a position, success depends upon attention and attentiveness. The absence of this quality is a predictor of trouble or failure.

Question: Consider a technical problem in your area of expertise. Describe how you solved it.

Interpretation: The answer to this question will shed light on your technical knowledge and problem-solving abilities.

Question: In checking your references, in what one area will your references tell me they have seen the greatest improvement in your performance? Why?

Interpretation: Your answer to this question will reflect what you believe to be your greatest weakness.

Question: List for me the leadership positions you have held, and what was it about them that broadened your leadership capabilities?

Interpretation: Your answer should mention demands placed on you in leadership roles. If you think they demonstrate major leadership responsibility, be sure to say so.

Question: What one individual has inspired you the most and what did this individual do that inspired you?

Interpretation: The answer to this question provides insight into how you want to be managed.

Question: What one aspect of your performance do you feel can be improved on and why?

Interpretation: This answer may reflect your last performance review. If it does, it's perfectly acceptable to say so and mention the steps you've initiated to address a perceived weakness.

Question: Have you ever been thrown into a situation in which you lacked the knowledge to do the job? What did you do? Give me an example.

Interpretation: Your interviewer will likely listen to the example you provide and compare it to what the individual who fills this role might experience in the position at hand.

Performance Issues

These questions focus on your performance in problem situations.

Question: Describe a major work-related problem you encountered and how you dealt with it.

Interpretation: This question challenges your self-assessment skills regarding what you believe to be a major work-related problem, as well as the approach to solving the problem. Your homework should give you insight into whether your performance history fits the company with which you are interviewing.

Question: Have you ever had to deal with an angry customer/client? What happened and how did you handle it?

Interpretation: If you are interviewing for a position that involves customer contact, this answer is important. Make it a good one. Be positive and calm when you explain how you defused the situation.

Question: If asked to solve a business problem that has no precedents, how would you go about it?

Interpretation: The objective of asking this question is to determine whether you have experience developing a logical problem-solving strategy. If not, where do you go for help?

Question: If you had to interview a technical individual in an area outside your realm of knowledge, how would you conduct the interview?

Interpretation: The answer to this question is an indicator of whether you know when, where, and how to gather information, or whether you are accustomed to winging it. Be sure your answer blends with the company's culture.

Question: At what point do you walk away from a business situation to re-focus yourself?

Interpretation: The answer to this question may give some insight as to how you deal with unpleasant situations. Sometimes you won't be able to walk away. . . .

Question: How do you deal with situations that affect your performance and are out of your control?

Interpretation: This question seeks to identify whether you take action or sit on the sidelines on issues that have an impact on your performance.

Question: Describe the steps you have taken to stay familiar with problem areas in your position.

Interpretation: This question points to the extent to which you use objective data or informal reports from colleagues, coworkers, or senior management.

Question: Tell me about a position in which there were constant surprises or unanticipated events. How did you deal with them?

Interpretation: Your answer to this question will be considered relative to the extent to which you developed plans and strategies so that surprises would not reoccur.

Question: What has been the most politically difficult work situation you have dealt with? What kinds of decisions did you make in that environment? Would you make those same decisions today?

Interpretation: This question seeks insight into your interpretation of a difficult political situation, how you handled sensitive issues, and what you learned from the experience.

Question: In your most recent position, what problems have you identified that had previously been overlooked?

Interpretation: Your answer to this question can help your interviewer determine whether you have or can develop a methodology for uncovering problems.

Decision Making

These questions focus on your decision-making ability.

Question: How do you make a decision from a leadership role, rather than a management role?

Interpretation: The answer to this question provides insight into your ability to lead without structure.

Question: Describe what you feel was the most successful business decision you have made.

Interpretation: This question seeks to understand what you believe is an important decision and your method of making decisions.

Question: What one important business decision would you re-think if given the chance?

Interpretation: The response to this question yields insight into your ability to learn from your mistakes and reevaluate situations.

Question: If I were to ask your supervisor what he or she thought was the major change in you during the period he or she managed you, what would I hear?

Interpretation: A safe answer is an example of a weakness that was pointed out in a recent performance review and that you are continuing to work on.

Question: Have you ever encountered a moral dilemma in a business setting? If so, describe it and how you dealt with it.

Interpretation: Very few individuals have not encountered a moral dilemma at some point on the job. Your interviewer will listen for what you feel was a moral dilemma and how it was handled.

Question: In your current position, cite an example of the types of decisions you make without consulting your manager. What is your level of authority?

Interpretation: The response to this question should provide information on the level of decision-making responsibility with which you are practiced and comfortable. Ideally, it matches that of the role for which you are interviewing.

Sales Recruitment Characteristics and Questions

Questions related to sales positions are targeted to garner insight into personality. How you answer is an indicator of your personality and temperament, and this information provides information about your likely approach to the sales process.

Goal-driven Characteristics

Top-performing sales professionals are, first and foremost, achievement oriented. Sales pros talk in terms of personal accomplishments. It's what makes (and keeps) them self-motivated. They have personal goals that are higher than those set for them by management. It never hurts to state, right up front, that you're goal driven.

Question: Tell me about some of your personal accomplishments and how your goals are established.

Interpretation: High producers keep close, frequent tabs on how they're doing, using their previous performance as a baseline. They compete against themselves. Their objective is to always improve on their earlier performance. Your answer should stress these characteristics of your approach to sales.

Question: How do you track how well you are doing?

Interpretation: Top producers keep close tabs on how they're doing, using their previous performance as a baseline. Their objective is to always improve on their earlier performance. Explain the tools you use to track your performance. If you've done your homework, you will mention the same tools used by the company with which you are interviewing.

Question: What happens when you lose a sale?

Interpretation: Top-performing salespeople don't give up. When they lose a sale, they find out why. They don't close the door on a lost opportunity. They make it their mission in life to recapture that sale. Explain how you accomplish this feat and you're halfway to the offer.

Question: How do you establish rapport in a selling situation?

Interpretation: True sales professionals can't be beat when it comes to their knowledge of details and technical performance statistics of the product or service they sell. As a result, their customers see them as consultants and problem solvers. It may be a challenge for you to be brief and concise as you speak to your knowledge of the products and services you sell, but try. You can always provide more details, but it's difficult to rewind the conversation once your interviewer has stopped listening.

Question: How strong is your knowledge of the details and technical distinguishers of your products and services, and how do you stay current?

Interpretation: The best salespeople don't wait to be told to take a training course or brush up on certain selling skills; they continually engage in self-advancement through self-training. They read sales and marketing books, trade journals, and newsletters. They attend seminars and they're always on the lookout for opportunities to learn new skills. The ones who really want to get ahead pursue the same kinds of information about their customers and their industries so they know how the products they're selling satisfy their customers' needs, particularly when the customers don't yet realize they have a need!

Question: Tell me about how you close a deal with a reluctant customer. How far are you willing to go?

Interpretation: This question seeks to determine whether you are assertive, which is a good thing, or aggressive, which is not a particularly welcome attribute for sales personnel who seek careers with companies that hope to maintain long and happy relationships with hard-won customers. Aggressive behavior is based on anger that achieves its objectives by demolishing obstacles. In a sales setting, that translates to a win/lose scenario if the goal is a sale and the prospect is blocking the way with objections; the salesperson might eventually win that sale but will likely lose the customer (and his or her job). Assertive people, on the other hand, hold their ground and seek a fair negotiated resolution that enables both sides to win. Make sure your presentation in the interview is clearly assertive but not aggressive.

Question: Describe a sales situation in which you took a stand and held your ground.

Interpretation: Professionals concentrate on the prospect's point of view with an intensity and respect that communicates their ability to understand the customer. This is the same sort of active listening you need to do during interviews.

Question: How would you describe your role and its impact on your company?

Interpretation: Top sales performers are conscious of their role in the organization. They are proud to be in a profession that makes the economy run. They support the job of everyone else in the company, and help clients overcome problems and meet their goals. They're happy to speak for hours about their impact on the company; you have only a minute or two to answer this question.

Question: How do you end a meeting with a prospect? What do you do to try to close the deal?

Interpretation: A salesperson hasn't finished his or her

job if he or she hasn't made a concerted effort to close the deal. Salespeople are, above all else, closers. How you, as a sales candidate, close the interview suggests how you'll close a sale. If you're not turned down, how and when will you follow up, assuming you don't hear from the interviewer after an agreed date? Mention that you ask what the next step will be and don't forget to ask the interviewer the same question. Professionals always plan that next step before they leave a client's office or a job interview.

Question: In what organizations or associations are you an active member?

Interpretation: Professional salespeople join every organization or association that will accept them as members. They do so to make contacts, network for other opportunities, and maintain awareness of what's going on in their customers' worlds. List the top six or seven organizations or associations in which you maintain membership. If you have or had a leadership role in any of them, be sure to mention it.

Question: What does it take to make you want to walk away from a business opportunity?

Interpretation: The answer to this question is an indicator of how far you are willing to go and what risk the company would encounter in order to make a sale. Yes, making the sale is important, but not at the expense of profit or reputation. Good salespeople don't sell products or services they know their companies can't deliver.

Question: If you were setting your own sales goals as well as those of the team selling our company's products, how would you go about establishing targets?

Interpretation: If you have had extensive experience in a goal-setting environment, this is an easy question. If you don't, you should have done enough homework to be able to answer this question. There are plenty of books on the market and information online about how sales goals should be set.

Question: Tell me about the training programs or seminars you've completed within the past two years.

Interpretation: The best salespeople do not wait to be told to take a training course or brush up on certain selling skills; they are continually engaged in self-advancement. They attend seminars and they are always on the lookout for opportunities to learn new skills. You should have no trouble listing the training you've taken recently.

Question: What do you consider to be important sales abilities when sitting down with a client?

Interpretation: Professional salespeople concentrate on the prospect's point of view with an intensity and respect that communicates their ability to understand (as opposed to simply agree with) the customer. This sort of active listening psychologically obligates the prospect to do the same. Demonstrate your awareness of this approach.

Prioritization Skills

Great salespeople have the ability to establish and maintain priorities. These questions are meant to solicit information about your prioritization skills.

Question: Give me an example of identifying a market requirement that was previously unnoticed. How did you present that opportunity to your management? What transpired as a result of your presentation?

Interpretation: Good salespeople don't like to let opportunity pass them by. The time and expense required to develop a new product or service, however, may far exceed the price a customer is willing to pay. If that cost can't be amortized across a wide range of customers (in other words, if it's a niche opportunity), the likelihood of that one-off product or service coming to fruition is slim. Good salespeople prioritize their opportunities (and potential opportunities) and make noise about only the truly important ones. Discuss a truly important market requirement, how you presented it to management, and the results of that presentation. Ideally, it should be something that was sold to both management and the customer.

Question: Would your manager describe you as the most creative individual in sales and marketing? Why or why not?

Interpretation: This is a loaded question in that, if you say yes, the next question will be proving it by examples. If no, the question then becomes why not? The safest answer is yes, as long as you have something with which to back it up.

Question: How do you manage your sales goals?

Interpretation: The simplest answer to this question is that you grab the low-hanging fruit first while you develop plans to pursue the less ripe fruit that will need time to mature.

Question: Describe in detail how you have managed and motivated your sales professionals. How much hand-holding do you do? Under what circumstances do you feel it is necessary for you to be involved in a sale?

Interpretation: Your answer to this question is an indicator of whether you manage at arm's length or feel the need to get involved in the details of each sale. Part of your answer may be related to the experience of your sales team, so if you have been getting involved in every sale and sense (or know from your homework) that this is not the type of salesperson the company is interested in hiring right now, be sure to explain your answer.

Question: What role have you played in setting goals for a marketing and sales team? Which goals, in your opinion, are the most difficult to achieve? When have you had to renegotiate a goal commitment?

Interpretation: Your answer to this question should indicate both commitment to a goal-setting process, awareness of what is achievable when setting goals, and willingness to be flexible if situations change.

Question: What percentage of your sales calls result in full presentations?

Interpretation: This question seeks to determine your ability to get through the gatekeepers and reach the decision maker.

Question: What kind of people do you like to sell to? To what kind of people do you not like to sell to? How do you manage to sell to these people?

Interpretation: Your answer to this question provides insight into your biases, ability to remain objective, and your skill to work beyond interpersonal difficulties that might arise during the sales process. A good answer would be that you enjoy selling to anyone who's willing to listen to your pitch, but enjoy the challenge of selling to those who aren't.

Question: What steps are involved in selling your company's product or service?

Interpretation: In asking this question, the interviewer is not so much interested in what you are selling but whether you are cognizant of the steps you follow. Are they presented logically? Will the same process be successful for the products or services of the company with which you are interviewing? If not, explain how you would alter your process to meet the needs of this company's product or service sales initiatives.

Question: How much time do you spend doing paperwork and other non-selling activities?

Interpretation: Paperwork is part of life. Your answer to this question should indicate you spend some small portion of your day or week on non-selling activities, including write-ups of sales calls and plans for pursuit of new opportunities.

Question: What aspect of your work do you consider crucial?

Interpretation: Your answer to this question should be management of people and achievement of business objectives.

Question: Which of your positions required the most attention to detail? How did you address the need and did you do anything unique to stay abreast of the detail?

Interpretation: Your answer to this question will probably be your best example of your attentiveness to detail and your approach to ensuring accuracy of detail. As long as it makes sense, that answer is fine.

Management Skills

Salespeople manage not only their teams but, at some level, their customers. These questions focus on the candidate's ability to manage people. The answers are particularly important if you are vying for a management position and will have to blend well with other managers.

Question: Give me some examples from your work experience that demonstrate your ability to organize and control people and work functions.

Interpretation: Your answer to this question should provide evidence that you have the ability to organize and control people and work functions. Your homework should provide clues as to whether your skills and approach fit the company's culture. Only in rare instances are lone wolves hired for management roles.

Question: As a manager, what have you done or are you currently doing that uniquely inspires your employees?

Interpretation: If you have unique or innovative ideas to manage and inspire employees, now is the time to sing your story.

Question: If I took a survey of your subordinates in recent years, how would they rate your management and leadership skills? On what would those ratings be based?

Interpretation: Part of a salesperson's job requires reading people. This question seeks to determine your ability to

215

understand how others perceive you relative to how you perceive and evaluate yourself. Your ratings should be based on your accomplishments.

Question: What is the most difficult management problem you've dealt with involving motivating your employees?

Interpretation: Your answer to this question should demonstrate creative, motivational ideas that would blend well with the company with which you are interviewing. Your homework should have provided clues on ideas they find valuable.

Question: In the last five years, what types of training have you received relative to employee management?

Interpretation: An indicator of a good manager is one who stretches his or her skills in the area of employee management, not just in business or technical areas. If your current or former employer didn't offer in-house training, be sure to mention where and how you pursued this type of training on your own.

Question: What motivational techniques have you developed over the years that have proven effective?

Interpretation: This question seeks to determine your level of initiative and creativity. Your answer should indicate whether you have experience developing your own motivational techniques and whether and how they've worked. Ideally, they should fit with those of the company with which you're interviewing. Even if they don't, the company might be interested in expanding its motivational techniques to include yours.

Achieving Business Objectives Skills

Sales positions are all about achieving business objectives. These questions focus on your experience achieving business objectives.

Question: How many business objectives do you establish each year and how do you decide on objectives?

Interpretation: Often business objectives are established at a level higher up the food chain than the salesperson. Still, the salesperson is obligated to achieve those objectives and a process must be put in place to do so. Your answer should demonstrate a logical, well thought out process for establishing objectives.

Question: What were some of the business objectives you've been challenged to achieve that you thought were a waste of time?

Interpretation: Your answer to this question provides insight into how you accept assignments, even if you disagree with them. The response is also a clue to how "manageable" you are and would be as an employee.

Question: Give me an example of a situation where your tenacity helped you to achieve a business objective.

Interpretation: Tenacity can be a good attribute for a salesperson because he or she may have to knock on many doors many times before being allowed entrance. Your response to this question is an indicator of your ability to overcome challenges with persistence.

Question: When have you found it necessary to follow up frequently on a project and what made you feel the need to do so?

Interpretation: This question seeks insight into the candidate's level of concentration and attentiveness to detail. Your interviewer will likely consider what you believe warrants attention relative to what you are likely to encounter at the company with which you are interviewing.

Management Style

These questions focus on your management style relative to subordinates.

Question: How do your employees approach you when there is a problem, either business-related or personal?

Interpretation: Your response to this question provides some indication as to the kind of management style and the level of relationship you establish with staff. Some companies prefer their managers to remain at arm's length and not befriend their staff, while others prefer a more collaborative, less hierarchical approach. Your homework should provide a clue into which approach is preferred at this company.

Question: What techniques have you developed as a part of your operating style to deal with changing situations?

Interpretation: Change is a constant. Your answer to this question provides insight into how you react to change. Often the way you react to change serves as an example to your team. If you have had to develop techniques to manage organizational changes, be sure to mention them.

Marketing Skills

These questions are targeted to assessing your skills if you are being considered for marketing positions.

Question: If given the opportunity, how would you go about setting up a strategic plan for a marketing effort?

Interpretation: This question speaks to strategic planning. Your answer will provide insight into your level of experience and expertise with strategic planning. There are plenty of books available on the subject and, if you are applying for a marketing role, it couldn't hurt to read a few of them.

Question: What has been your greatest challenge in marketing planning and how did you overcome it?

Interpretation: This is a straightforward question aimed at probing your marketing background. There is no right or wrong answer.

Question: Are you aware of possible future trends, technologies, or market opportunities that will allow you to create that next big winner or killer application? What are some of the trends you see?

Interpretation: This question seeks to assess whether you are intellectually curious and innovative. People in marketing drive the company's growth and are known for being innovative. If you're not, you might be ill suited for this occupation.

Question: What plans or back-up products do you have that can compete with existing competitors' new products and with new competitors of similar products?

Interpretation: This question speaks to your ability to anticipate competitors' moves. You should be aware of newcomers to the market, as well as the next big product likely to emerge on the horizon.

Question: What contingency plans do you have in place if your largest one or two customers were to stop purchasing your products or offerings?

Interpretation: Marketing candidates should show ingenuity and capability to investigate current trends in the marketplace. They always have another idea up their sleeves or on the drawing boards.

Question: Do you know how your company's operating efficiencies, costs, and pricing structures compare to those of your competitors? What other questions must you ask continuously to evaluate your company and effectively compete in today's marketplace?

Interpretation: This question seeks to identify whether you work methodically with facts, figures, and intelligence to ensure competitiveness in the marketplace. You can't fake this answer and the wrong one could end the interview. Be prepared.

Question: Based on your research of this position and markets, what steps and approach would you take to establish a new marketing focus? What would be your timeframe?

Interpretation: Your answer to this question should demonstrate the types of intelligence you have developed and what you view as critical steps in establishing a new focus.

Question: In your past management roles, what were the major reasons that strategic marketing was not effective or as effective as it should have been? What did you do to correct the problem?

Interpretation: Your answer to this question is a window on your past experience with difficult marketing issues and the types of actions taken to solve those issues. Your interviewer will likely consider whether these are similar to those at the company with which you are interviewing. If you were able to succeed in the past, you should be able to repeat that success.

Question: Think of a new breakthrough technology. If this were your discovery, how would you market it? What existing technology would your discovery displace, and why?

Interpretation: The answer to this question provides insight into your ability to think on your feet. Can you?

Question: Imagine you have discovered a previously unmet market requirement. How would you present the opportunity to your management?

Interpretation: Your answer to this question is indicative of your ability to analyze the market, recognize opportunities, and present a well thought out plan to capitalize on the opportunity. Your answer should give proof that you understand which opportunities are worth pursuing and which are more costly than the revenues they would likely yield.

Using LinkedIn

Today, being well connected is a requirement in building and maintaining a career. LinkedIn with its forty million members is one of the premier "relation building" Web sites. The best thing is it doesn't take a lot of time to master the many options and customize them for your personal use.

To Start:

1. Once a member, focus on the quality of your information you post on yourself. For LinkedIn to become a positive tool for you, your information, i.e., resume, career details, has to be well written to stand out—and the more detail the better. One mistake many users make is just listing their current position. The mindset needs to be one of writing about what makes you unique, and then update this information as often as possible.

2. Recommendations: LinkedIn allow users to add personal recommendations to their profile. The method of getting recommendations is to contact other users you may know and ask them (based on their backgrounds) to write a recommendation for you. All recruiters when sourcing for candidates review these recommendations. This is in a way a reference check. The problem with recommendations is that if they are not well written (some are just faint praise) and from an accomplished individual, they fall flat.

3. Utilizing LinkedIn, especially when seeking a new position, requires thinking through the range of possible contacts before starting to contact individuals. LinkedIn allows anyone to look up any person by name or find individuals by skill bases, locations, expertise, etc. Each profile normally has the individual's work history in some form, as well as contacts they have and personal recommendations from others on their accomplishments. This information is useful when trying to establish a personal contact.

   Networking using LinkedIn is the best method to secure a position. It is far superior to using the Internet boards for job leads. People hire people who they feel they know, or when they trust the referrer. Start with making a list of individuals you know that have influence. Personal friends who do not have stature or influence cannot help in a job search.

   When contacting prospects, be aware if you are not offering them anything of value in connecting with you, chances are they will reject the invitation. Doing an e-mail blast out to members of your business sector or professional level may cause LinkedIn to flag you for spamming. At the bottom of every profile is what the member is interested in in terms of accepting contacts.

   An expensive option, but an excellent one for networking is becoming a Premium Member. The Premium Account allows you to send fifty e-mails a month to other members, as well as simplifies the process to get and accept introductions. In running a job search campaign or establishing and getting contacts, the Premium Account vastly speeds up the process allowing a multitude of contacts at the same time, which is not possible otherwise.

4. Once you are online and using LinkedIn, do a search for individuals in your career sector first. Then with every member that appears, drill down in their contact lists to see if anyone could be of help to you. This takes time, but it's well worth the effort. Assuming there are a few

at the right level in organizations of interest, record the contact information for later use.

5. Understand not all contacts will reply, but many will. All members are seeking to expand their network of contacts. A note of caution: when contacted by another member to linkup, check out the individual's profile before accepting; always make sure this is someone who will enhance your contacts list. These individuals then become a resource for you after you have established a relationship.

6. Once your list is completed, do twenty contacts at a time to get started. Compose a <u>short</u> e-mail to each contact. The best way to do this is to write the e-mail and then paste it into the e-mail message box of the candidate. Take the time to wordsmith the message; the purpose of the e-mail is to start a relationship.

For example:

Hi

I am new to LinkedIn and work in the same industry as you do. I thought I would drop you a note to connect and possibly exchange information on the industry/sector. I have had some interesting conversations with others who share our business interest and thought maybe an informational network might be of interest to you too.

I look forward to connecting with you and exchanging information.

Sincerely, {end email}

Some things you may not know:

1. **Get to know the "advanced search" functions.** This is a great and probably underused tool. The page allows you to narrow a search with industry categories and titles, but the most handy search weapon is the keyword search. Say you're looking for a new job in your industry

and you want to find out about corporate culture at NetApp. Type in "sales" and "NetApp" (you can use quote marks to search for a phrase and the connectors "and" and "or"), and you'll get two categories of people who define themselves as such: those in your network of connections, and those in the wider LinkedIn universe.

2. **Check out a person's history.** You can learn a lot about someone on their profile page; if they let you (LinkedIn's "accounts and settings" function lets you set privacy controls). For instance, a little dinky called the "one-click reference" at the top of the page tells you all the people on the network who worked with the person at the company. That's very useful in expanding your business contacts.

3. Another helpful option is that members can ask questions of their network and/or the LinkedIn universe on the "answers" page. If you're researching a subject and want to expand on your information base, this is a great tool.

4. **Connect your e-mail contacts with LinkedIn's.** Under "my contacts," there's a tool on the right that allows LinkedIn to search your Gmail or Yahoo accounts to see if anybody you've ever e-mailed is also a member. That's an easy way to build up your network without tediously typing in everybody's e-mail.

5. **Build a network without making networking your full-time job.** To use LinkedIn well, you need at least thirty connections. But, as I previously mentioned, this doesn't mean you should connect to every individual who sends you an invitation. LinkedIn works best when you connect to your top sources, important industry contacts, coworkers, and people who know you well. These are the people who can help you do your job or find new opportunities.

6. **Need an expert, the Advance Search tool** feature, is the most powerful tool you can use on LinkedIn. You can search for any combination of keywords, job title, company, location, industry, and you can sort by "degrees away from you" to find people close to you in your network. This is a great way to find experts in almost any field or subject matter. You can also track down executives at companies.

7. **Check out trends.** LinkedIn Answers has a search box that allows you to search the archives. This is a great way to search for sources. A search for keyword will likely find you the buzz around the product. A great way to get ideas is to pursue through the various categories of LinkedIn Answers to find out what people are saying about topics and trends.

8. Increase your visibility by adding connections, thereby increasing the likelihood that people will see your profile first when they're searching for someone to hire or do business with. In addition to appearing at the top of search results, people would much rather work with people who their friends know and trust.

9. As previously mentioned, improving your connectability is key. Most new users put only their current company in their profile. By doing so, they severely limit their ability to connect with people. You should fill out your profile in as much detail as possible, include past companies, education, affiliations, and activities.

10. Improve your Google Page Rank. LinkedIn allows you to make your profile information available for search engines to index. Since LinkedIn profiles receive a fairly high Page Rank in Google, this is a good way to influence what people see when they search for you. To do this, create a public profile and select "Full View."

11. Do company reference checks. LinkedIn's reference check tool allows users to input a company name and the years the person worked at the company to search for references. Your search will find the people who worked at the company during the same time period. Since references provided by a candidate will generally be glowing, this is a good way to get more balanced data. You can also check up on the company itself by finding the person who used to have the job that you're interviewing for. Do this by searching for job title and company, but be sure to uncheck "Current titles only." By contacting people who used to hold the position, you can get the inside scoop on the job, manager, and growth potential.

12. Expand your job search. Use LinkedIn's advanced search to find people with educational and work experience like yours to see where they work. For example, a software manager would use search keywords such as "Software," "Microsoft," and "Java" to find out where other software types with these skills work.

13. Get a leg up on your next interview; you can use LinkedIn to find the people that you're meeting. Knowing that you went to the same school, play the same sports, or share acquaintances will better prepare you for the small talk part of the interview.

14. Check out the health of a company by performing an advanced search for company name and uncheck the "Current Companies Only" box. This will enable you to scrutinize the rate of turnover and whether key people are abandoning ship. Former employees usually give more candid opinions about a company's prospects than someone who's still on board.

15. Check out the health of an industry if you're thinking of investing or working in a sector. Use LinkedIn to find people who worked for competitors—or even better, companies who failed.

16. Check out startups; you can see people in your network who are initiating new startups by doing an advanced search for a range of keywords such as "stealth" or "new startup."

17. Since Linkedin is a live resource, its information changes by the hour; what was not available yesterday may be posted today. Check LinkedIn as often as you check your e-mail and also check on your profile page to see who is accessing your profile: it's on the left hand side of your profile. This is one of the indicators of how your networking is going.

Executive Search Firms

Rather than list all the firms in the United States for you, here is the best resource.

The Directory of Executive and Professional Recruiters 2009–2010
"The Industry Bible" — The Wall Street Journal

13,000+ recruiters • 6,000+ firm locations
FREE access to the latest online listings

The Directory of Executive and Professional Recruiters, otherwise known as the famed "Red Book," is the premier junior, senior and executive-level job seekers guide for researching and contacting recruiting firms that will best facilitate their career goals.

Trusted by job seekers for over thirty-five years, the recruiting industry's most highly regarded, comprehensive source of key data and contacts offers a new look and fresh approach for 2009–2010. Kennedy's *Directory of Executive Recruiters* will now be called *The Directory of Executive and Professional Recruiters* to more accurately depict its vast scope.

Five easy-to-search indexes include:
- 84 Job Placement Areas (type of job)
- 120+ Industries (type of company)
- 400+ Individual Recruiter Specialties
- Geographical (by city and state)
- A–Z Listing

LaVergne, TN USA
10 May 2010
182203LV00002B/40/P